English Lessons Through *Literature*

Level 2

Kathy Jo DeVore

barefoot ragamuffin curricula

www.barefootmeandering.com
veritas • gnaritas • libertas

Copyright © 2014 by Kathy Jo DeVore. The eBook version may be printed for the use of one household and may not be resold. The print version may not be reproduced.

Scripture quotations taken from the New American Standard Bible®, Copyright © 1960, 1962, 1963, 1968, 1971, 1972, 1973, 1975, 1977, 1995 by The Lockman Foundation. Used by permission.

Clipart images Copyright © GraphicsFactory.com

liberis meis

Table of Contents

Introduction 11

Level 2 Literature List 19

1. Definition: Noun: Person 21
2. Common and Proper Nouns 24
3. Noun: Place; Picture Study: A Shepherdess and Her Flock 27
4. Noun: Place 29
5. Noun: Thing 32
6. Narration: The Young Crab and His Mother 34
7. The Months of the Year 36
8. Noun: Idea 39
9. Quotations; Picture Study: Peasants Bringing Home a Calf Born in the Fields 43
10. Name and Initials 45
11. Definition: Verb: Action Verb 49
12. Narration: The Boy and the Filberts 51
13. Writing Dates 53
14. Quotations 55
15. Invisible Action Verbs; Picture Study: The Knitting Lesson 59
16. Definition: Pronoun 61
17. First Person Pronouns 64
18. Narration: The Crow and the Pitcher 66
19. First Person Pronouns 68
20. Abbreviations: Months, Streets 71
21. Capitalization; Picture Study: The Bouquet of Margueritas 75
22. Second Person Pronouns 77
23. Definition: Homophones 80
24. Narration: The Kid and the Wolf 83
25. The Four Seasons 84
26. Second Person Pronouns 87

27.	Abbreviations: States; Picture Study: Woman Baking Bread	91
28.	Addresses	93
29.	Third Person Singular Pronouns	96
30.	Narration: The Boy Bathing	98
31.	Third Person Plural Pronouns	100
32.	Phone Numbers	102
33.	State of Being Verbs; Picture Study: Woman Hanging Her Laundry	105
34.	Contractions	107
35.	Review: Capitalization	111
36.	Narration: The Boys and the Frogs	114
37.	The Days of the Week	116
38.	State of Being Verbs; Review: Pronouns	118
39.	Contractions; Picture Study: Fresh Eggs	121
40.	Linking Verbs	124
41.	Linking Verbs	126
42.	Narration: The Fox and the Grapes	128
43.	Abbreviations: Titles of Respect	130
44.	Review: Name, Address, and Phone Number	132
45.	Quotations: Review, Punctuation; Picture Study: Girl Carrying a Basket	135
46.	Definition: Conjunction	137
47.	Helping Verbs	140
48.	Narration: The Farmer and His Sons	143
49.	Linking Verbs and Helping Verbs	145
50.	Quotations: Punctuation	148
51.	Helping Verbs; Picture Study: On the Fence	151
52.	Letter from Neverland	153
53.	Addressing an Envelope	157
54.	Narration: The Ants and the Grasshopper	160
55.	Definition: Sentence; Declarative Sentences	162
56.	Definition: Adjective	165
57.	Interrogative Sentences; Picture Study: Snap the Whip	169

58.	Exclamatory Sentences	171
59.	Imperative Sentences	173
60.	Narration: The Wolf and the Crane	176
61.	Letter to/from Mr. Toad	178
62.	Addressing an Envelope	181
63.	Review: Sentence Types; Picture Study: The Country School	185
64.	Possessive Case	187
65.	Review: Adjectives	190
66.	Narration: The Hare and the Tortoise	192
67.	Commas in a Series	194
68.	Predicate Adjectives	197
69.	Possessive Case; Homophones; Picture Study: Sponge Fishing, Nassau	201
70.	The Ten Commandments	204
71.	Review: Nouns, Pronouns, Adjectives, Verbs	207
72.	Hercules and the Wagoner	209
73.	Definition: Preposition	211
74.	Prepositions	213
75.	Definition: Interjection; Picture Study: Fifteen Sunflowers in a Vase	217
76.	Prepositions	219
77.	Interjections	221
78.	Narration: Belling the Cat	223
79.	Prepositions	225
80.	Definition: Adverb	229
81.	Prepositions; Picture Study: First Steps	233
82.	Adverbs	235
83.	Prepositions	237
84.	Narration: The Bundle of Sticks	239
85.	Adverbs	241
86.	Review: Prepositions	244
87.	Homophones; Picture Study: Irises	247
88.	Prepositions and Adverbs	249

89.	Review: Nouns, Adjectives, Verbs, Adverbs	252
90.	Narration: The Lion and the Mouse	254
91.	Review: Sentence Types	257
92.	Definition: Antonyms	260
93.	A Poem, a Fable, and Copywork; Picture Study: The Starry Night	263
94.	Articles	265
95.	Antonyms	268
96.	Narration: The Shepherd Boy and the Wolf	270
97.	Review: Nouns, Adjectives, Verbs, Adverbs	272
98.	Review: Interjections	274
99.	Review: Conjunctions; Picture Study: Van Gogh's Room at Arles	277
100.	Review: Contractions, Homophones	279
101.	Definition: Synonyms	282
102.	Narration: The Arab and His Camel	285
103.	Nouns and Pronouns as Adjectives	288
104.	Nouns and Pronouns as Adjectives	291
105.	Review: Synonyms; Picture Study: Village Street and Stairs	295
106.	Review: Commas in a Series	297
107.	The Eight Parts of Speech	300
108.	Narration: The Town Mouse and the Country Mouse	302

Appendix A: Memory Work	305
Appendix B: Memorizing Prepositions, Pros and Cons	307

Introduction

After more than seven years of homeschooling, I've come to a conclusion: While I often regret the purchase of curricula, I rarely regret the purchase of quality books.

It may seem ironic, then, that I've chosen to write a grammar curriculum for young children. I believe absolutely in copywork, narration, and dictation for instilling values, promoting memorization, and teaching spelling and writing. Yet, in the early years I relied on grammar texts for young children that taught using sentences manufactured for the sole purpose of demonstrating grammatical concepts.

The real irony lies in focusing on quality literature in every area *except* the teaching of the grammar and mechanics of the English language. While I believe the best way to teach grammar and mechanics is through literature and that no curriculum is needed for this, I also believe the easiest way to do this is through a series of lessons based on literature that can be repeated with each child. So here we are.

The reasoning behind manufactured sentences is often that in using real sentences from literature, children will encounter advanced concepts which they have not yet learned. However, once upon a time, every elementary student was a toddler just learning to speak. He sometimes confused "my" and "me," he might have formed plurals incorrectly, and he made any number of other grammatical errors. A great many of us found these errors very cute, even while we corrected them. What we didn't do was simplify our speech to the child's level of understanding, knowing that he would learn best by exposure to correctly spoken language.

And so it is with teaching grammar and mechanics. When I first began narration with my oldest son, we used an old retelling of Aesop with its more difficult syntax and vocabulary rather than using a modern, simplified retelling of Aesop. I followed this pattern with my second son in his turn. Instead of being confused, both of my sons amazed me by incorporating those advanced concepts into their narrations.

Children learn by imitating. It is up to us to insure what they come into contact with is worthy of imitation.

K. J. D., 2009.

Schedule and Readiness

This book was previously published as *Language Lessons Through Literature.*

Both levels of this program are intended as three-day-per-week lessons over thirty-six weeks, for a total of 108 lessons per year. Each lesson includes a literature selection to be read aloud, a poem, and either an Aesop's fable or a picture study.

Level 1 is intended for a first grade child who is ready for copywork and is beginning to read fluently. Level 2 is intended for a second grade child or for older children in need of remediation. Completion of Level 1 is not a prerequisite for Level 2.

Purpose and Necessary Resources

Level 1 is an intentionally light program. First grade should be a time for getting children comfortable with reading and handwriting. Most young children are simply not ready for more advanced grammar, and the grammar for which they are ready can be taught very quickly when they are just a little older. Although children can begin learning the parts of speech in the first grade, the simple fact is that one can take two years beginning in first grade to teach the parts of speech, or one can take one year beginning in second grade to teach the parts of speech. It's simply more efficient to wait until the child is truly ready, and it leaves more time to focus on reading and handwriting during first grade. An advanced child—one who was reading and writing comfortably in Kindergarten—might be best served by skipping Level 1 and going straight into Level 2, or by using Level 1 in Kindergarten.

The focus of Level 1 is to begin teaching usage and mechanics of the English language through copywork. Although I have written lessons for many (but not all) of the Level 1 lessons, the real lessons are truly the copywork selections. It is in copywork that children will learn and internalize proper spelling, capitalization, and punctuation while practicing handwriting. The lessons that I've written for Level 1 merely point out and reinforce concepts to the child before he begins his copywork. Children are introduced to punctuation marks, quotations, and contractions; they then practice writing them.

In Level 2, the child learns the parts of speech as well as lists of helping verbs, prepositions, etc. Examples and exercises consist of a sentence or passage from the literature or from a poem. In the exercises, the child takes what he has learned from the lesson and demonstrates understanding. The repetition necessary for mastery comes from constant review in the exercises, not from long exercises.

I have occasionally simplified or modified sentences to avoid confusion, but I have tried to keep this to a minimum. Particularly in Level 1, some sentences have been shortened to make them a more appropriate length for copywork. Since all of the literature selections are old, and many are British, spelling and punctuation have been modified as necessary.

The literature selections in this book are intended to be read aloud to the child; this program does not cover reading instruction. In addition, spelling is not taught explicitly, so a formal spelling program, if desired, should be supplied separately.

Literature Selections

The literature suggested in this book is in the public domain in the United States and the full text of each story and book can be found online. Most are also available as audio books. A complete reading list appears at the beginning of each level.

Since most of the examples and part of the daily copywork come directly from the literature, reading the literature is an important component of this program. However, there is certainly room to skip books that the child does not like. Fairy tales may be disturbing to some children, and it is up to the parents to determine whether or not a recommended resource is right for their family. My homeschooling motto has long been, "Use the curriculum; don't let the curriculum use you." I recommend the motto more highly than I recommend any of the literature selections in this book.

I do recommend reading the literature prior to the lesson. The examples and the copywork almost always come from the reading selection from that day.

Copywork

This book contains a great deal of copywork. From the middle of Level 1 through Level 2, most weeks have five pages of copywork consisting of one to four lines per page for each week: three pages from the literature selection, one from the poetry selection, and one containing a maxim or Bible verse. This amount of copywork would have made my oldest son cry. My second son wanted more copywork than this. If you find this is too much copywork for your child, there are several options:

1. Skip part of the copywork. Decide which portions of the copywork are most important to your goals, and have your child do only those.

2. If you'd rather have your child do all of the copywork, have the child do the copywork portions five days a week instead of three. This would be one page of copywork per day.

3. Have your child do copywork in the morning and again in the afternoon. If your child is doing copywork three days a week, this would be one page in the morning and one page in the afternoon twice a week, with only one page of copywork on the last lesson day of the week. If your child is doing copywork five days per week, this would only be half a page at each sitting.

Narrations

Narrations occur every two weeks throughout both levels. Once the child is comfortable with narrating, you can include narration exercises from history and science reading as well. Each level includes ninety of Aesop's fables that could also be used for additional narration practice if desired.

Level 1 begins with picture narrations. After the instructor reads the fable, the child is asked to draw a picture of the story and then tell his instructor about the picture. During the second half of the year, he will begin standard narrations.

The standard narrations at the end of Level 1 and throughout Level 2 start with the shortest Aesop's fables and gradually increase in length. The procedure for doing the

narrations is quite simple: After the instructor reads the fable, the child tells the story back to his instructor
in his own words while the instructor writes the story down for the child. Remember that the child is learning a brand new skill and may not understand exactly what is expected of him. Prompting him with questions helps. Ask questions such as, "What happened first?" and, "Then what happened?" Help him get the details of the story in the proper order. Since the instructor is doing the writing for the child, the child has no need to worry about spelling or punctuation. At this stage, I correct nothing more than grammatical errors and, occasionally, a detail from the story.

In Level 2, part of the narration will be printed or written for the child to use as copywork for that day.

Approached this way, narrations follow a logical progression. Narrations first start with something the child is probably already doing: drawing pictures and explaining them. Next the child begins telling the story without the picture, though he may certainly draw a picture to illustrate his narration. Then, he begins copying his own words. Finally, he will begin writing the story down himself without orally narrating it first. This final stage is not covered in this book.

Memory Work

Both levels include lists to memorize, and Level 2 includes many definitions to memorize as well. In Level 1, the lists to learn are included in the lessons with instructions for memorization, and reviews are included in the lessons as well. However, poetry and Bible verses are not included in the lessons for memorization. In Level 2, grammatical concepts and lists are introduced in the lessons, but should be memorized separately. Grammar memory work is included in Appendix A for quick and easy review.

I recommend a memory card system for Bible and poetry.

I do not specify which poems to memorize. My suggestion is to begin memorizing the first poem of the level. When that is memorized, choose one of the poems that the child particularly liked from the preceding lessons, or one that you feel is particularly important, and begin memorizing it. Continue in this fashion throughout the year. There are 108 poems in each level, giving everyone a good selection from which to choose. For Christians, there is a Bible verse to be used as copywork every two weeks beginning in Lesson 38 of Level 1. I advise memorizing these verses unless you already have memory verses from church or a Bible study program.

We use 5 x 8 index cards because there are binders available to hold them, but smaller index cards work just as well. Have dividers for three sections: Current, Short Term Review, and Long Term Review. One side of the card should have the title of the card (i.e. John 3:16, Definition of a Noun, Clouds by Christina Rossetti, etc.). The reverse has the memory work.

Cards in the Current section should be read three times a day until the passage has been memorized. The card can then move to the Short Term Review section, and that section can be reviewed once a week. Once the child has successfully recited a card several weeks in a row, it can go into the Long Term Review section for review once a month. You can also color code the cards by subject or topic.

Picture Study

All pictures of paintings in this book are, of necessity, black and white. I highly recommend searching online for color copies of the art to view online or print for studying. Color copies of the paintings are included in the optional workbook file for convenience.

Optional Workbook

The suggested exercises and copywork are included in this book, so the workbook is truly optional. The benefits of purchasing the workbook are:

1. The workbook is a file that may be printed out for all the children in your family. It may not be resold.

2. The copywork is already typed in a handwriting font so that you don't have to type or write it for the child to copy. There are several popular handwriting styles from which to choose, and you get them all because you shouldn't have to buy a new workbook if you change handwriting styles with the next child.

Color copies of the artwork are available as a free download. Very light black and white copies of the artwork are included as coloring pages.

Level Two

Level 2 Literature List

All the literature selections suggested herein are in the public domain in the United States of America and are probably available at your local library. The complete texts can also be found online from Project Gutenberg (www.gutenberg.org) and/or the Baldwin Project (www.mainlesson.com). Most are available as audio books, and free audio book versions may be found online from LibriVox (www.librivox.org).

The Wonderful Wizard of Oz by L. Frank Baum

The Blue Fairy Book by Andrew Lang (13 stories)

Peter Pan by J. M. Barrie

The Wind in the Willows by Kenneth Grahame

Alice's Adventures in Wonderland by Lewis Carroll

Through the Looking-Glass and What Alice Found There by Lewis Carroll

A Wonder-Book for Girls and Boys by Nathaniel Hawthorne

The Aesop's fables in Level 2 are from *The Aesop for Children* illustrated by Milo Winter and *Aesop's Fables* by J. H. Stickney.

1. Definition: Noun: Person

- The Wonderful Wizard of Oz, Chapter 1

A noun is the name of a
person, place, thing, or idea.

Everybody and everything has a name. We call those words nouns. A noun is the name a person, place, thing, or idea. We're going to start by looking at the first part of that definition: A noun is the name of a person.

You are a person. Are you a boy or a girl? **Boy** and **girl** are both nouns because they are names for people.

In your family, there are many kinds of people. You might have a **mother**, a **father**, a **grandmother**, and a **grandfather**. These words are all nouns that name people. Can you think of other nouns that name people in your family?

In *The Wonderful Wizard of Oz*, Dorothy is a little girl who lives with her aunt and uncle. Names for people are nouns. Since **Dorothy, girl, aunt,** and **uncle** are all names for people, they are all nouns. In the following sentence from *The Wonderful Wizard of Oz*, the names for people are underlined:

> <u>Dorothy</u> lived in the midst of the great Kansas prairies, with <u>Uncle Henry</u>, who was a <u>farmer</u>, and <u>Aunt Em</u>, who was the farmer's <u>wife</u>.

Clouds
by Christina Rossetti

White sheep, white sheep,
On a blue hill,
When the wind stops
You all stand still;
When the wind blows
You walk away slow,
White sheep, white sheep,
Where do you go?

Your first poem is called "Clouds" by Christina Rossetti. To what does she compare the clouds? What is the blue hill?

Mercury and the Woodman

An Aesop's Fable

A poor Woodman was cutting down a tree near the edge of a deep pool in the forest. It was late in the day and the Woodman was tired. He had been working since sunrise and his strokes were not so sure as they had been early that morning. Thus it happened that the axe slipped and flew out of his hands into the pool.

The Woodman was in despair. The axe was all he possessed with which to make a living, and he had not money enough to buy a new one. As he stood wringing his hands and weeping, the god Mercury suddenly appeared and asked what the trouble was. The Woodman told what had happened, and straightway the kind Mercury dived into the pool. When he came up again he held a wonderful golden axe.

"Is this your axe?" Mercury asked the Woodman.

"No," answered the honest Woodman, "that is not my axe."

Mercury laid the golden axe on the bank and sprang back into the pool. This time he brought up an axe of silver, but the Woodman declared again that his axe was just an ordinary one with a wooden handle.

Mercury dived down for the third time, and when he came up again he had the very axe that had been lost.

The poor Woodman was very glad that his axe had been found and could not thank the kind god enough. Mercury was greatly pleased with the Woodman's honesty.

"I admire your honesty," he said, "and as a reward you may have all three axes, the gold and the silver as well as your own."

The happy Woodman returned to his home with his treasures, and soon the story of his good fortune was known to everybody in the village. Now there were several Woodmen in the village who believed that they could easily win the same good fortune. They hurried out into the woods, one here, one there, and hiding their axes in the bushes, pretended they had lost them. Then they wept and wailed and called on Mercury to help them.

And indeed, Mercury did appear, first to this one, then to that. To each one he showed an axe of gold, and each one eagerly claimed it to be the one he had lost. But Mercury did not give them the golden axe. Oh no! Instead he gave them each a hard whack over the head with it and sent them home. And when they returned next day to look for their own axes, they were nowhere to be found.

Honesty is the best policy.

Exercise

In your workbook, underline the nouns that name people from this passage:

Suddenly Uncle Henry stood up.

"There's a cyclone coming, Em," he called to his wife.

[Note to instructor: Some children may recognize "he" and "his" as words naming people. This is a good thing! It means that the child firmly grasped the lesson on words that name people. If your child does, you can point out that these are special words called pronouns, and we'll begin discussing pronouns in Lesson 16.]

Copywork

Literature

"There's a cyclone coming, Em," he called to his wife.

Poetry—Clouds

White sheep, white sheep,
On a blue hill,
When the wind stops
You all stand still;

2. Common and Proper Nouns

- The Wonderful Wizard of Oz, Chapter 2

A noun is the name of a person, place, thing, or idea.

Think of the different people you have met. You know men and women, boys and girls. **Men, women, boys,** and **girls** are all nouns because these words name people. Besides your family, you might know a doctor whom you see when you are sick and a librarian who helps you find books. **Doctor** and **librarian** are both nouns because these words name people, too. Can you think of some other nouns that name people?

Dorothy is a little girl. **Girl** is a common noun. A common noun is a noun that can be common to many people. Dorothy is a little girl, but so are many other people. But Dorothy also has a special name all her own: Dorothy! **Dorothy** is a proper noun. When we talk about Dorothy, we're not talking about just any little girl, but one special little girl. When we write someone's special, proper name, we begin it with a capital letter.

Look at this sentence from *The Wonderful Wizard of Oz* again:

> <u>Dorothy</u> lived in the midst of the great Kansas prairies, with <u>Uncle Henry</u>, who was a <u>farmer</u>, and <u>Aunt Em</u>, who was the farmer's <u>wife</u>.

Dorothy lived with Uncle Henry and Aunt Em. **Dorothy, Uncle Henry,** and **Aunt Em** are proper nouns because they name specific people. Uncle Henry is a farmer. **Farmer** is a common noun because there are many farmers. Aunt Em is Uncle Henry's wife. **Wife** is also a common noun because many women are also wives.

What is your special, proper name? What are the special, proper names for the people in your family?

Whole Duty of Children
by Robert Louis Stevenson

A child should always say what's true,
And speak when he is spoken to,
And behave mannerly at table:
At least as far as he is able.

The Cock and the Jewel
An Aesop's Fable

A Cock was busily scratching and scraping about to find something to eat for himself and his family, when he happened to turn up a precious jewel that had been lost by its owner.

"Aha!" said the Cock. "No doubt you are very costly and he who lost you would give a great deal to find you. But as for me, I would choose a single grain of barleycorn before all the jewels in the world."

Precious things are without value to those who cannot prize them.

Exercise

In your workbook, underline the nouns that name people from this passage:

"Who is Aunt Em?" inquired the little old woman.

"She is my aunt who lives in Kansas, where I came from."

Which nouns are common, and which nouns are proper?

Copywork

Literature

"Who is Aunt Em?" inquired the little old woman.

Bible—Romans 12:21

Do not be overcome by evil, but overcome evil with good.

A Shepherdess and Her Flock by Jean-Francois Millet

Picture Study

1. Read the title and the name of the artist. Study the picture for several minutes, then put the picture away.

2. Describe the picture.

3. Look at the picture again. Do you notice any details that you missed before? What do you like or dislike about this painting? Does it remind you of anything?

3. Noun: Place; Picture Study: A Shepherdess and Her Flock

- The Wonderful Wizard of Oz, Chapter 3

A noun is the name of a person, place, thing, or idea.

Nouns are the names for more than just people. The names of places are also nouns.

Do you like to go to the park or the zoo? Do you ever go to the store? **Park, zoo,** and **store** are all nouns that name places. These words are all common nouns because there are many parks, zoos, and stores. Each park, zoo, and store can also have its own special, proper name as well.

Think of some other places you like to go, or places you would like to go. Would you like to go see an ocean? **Ocean** is a common noun, but **Atlantic Ocean** is a proper noun because it is the special, proper name of a specific ocean. Would you like to go to a mountain? **Mountain** is a common noun, but **Rocky Mountains** is a proper noun because it is the name for a specific chain of mountains. Would you like to go see a canyon? **Canyon** is a common noun, but **Grand Canyon** is a proper noun because it is the name of a specific canyon. Remember that proper nouns always begin with a capital letter.

Dorothy lived on a farm. **Farm** is a noun, too, because it is the name of a place. Is **farm** a common noun or a proper noun?

Think of some more places. Which names are common nouns and which names are proper nouns?

Faults
by Sara Teasdale

They came to tell your faults to me,
They named them over one by one,
I laughed aloud when they were done;
I knew them all so well before, -
Oh they were blind, too blind to see
Your faults had made me love you more.

Exercise

In your workbook, underline all of the nouns that name people and places from this passage:

> "Come along, Toto," she said. "We will go to the Emerald City and ask the Great Oz how to get back to Kansas again."

Which nouns are common and which are proper?

Copywork

Literature

> "We will go to the Emerald City and ask the Great Oz how to get back to Kansas again."

4. Noun: Place

- The Wonderful Wizard of Oz, Chapter 4

A noun is the name of a person, place, thing, or idea.

Where do you live? Do you live in a town or a city? **Town** and **city** are names for places. They are common nouns because there are many towns and cities. Each town and city also has its own special, proper name, just like each child has his own special, proper name. What is the name of the town or city in which you live?

Your town or city is in a state, and the states are all in a country. **State** and **country** are common nouns; there are many states and countries. Our country is called the United States of America. **United States of America** is a proper noun since it's our country's special, proper name. There are fifty states in our country, and each has its own special, proper name, too.

Because they are proper nouns, the names of towns, cities, countries, and states always begin with capital letters.

In which state do you live? Were you born in that state, or were you born in another state?

In *The Wonderful Wizard of Oz*, Dorothy lived in the state named Kansas. Kansas is a proper noun. It's not the name of just any state, but of one particular state. Dorothy is traveling to the Emerald City. Is Emerald City a proper noun or a common noun?

Can you think of other names for places?

Piping Down the Valleys Wild
by William Blake

Piping down the valleys wild,
Piping songs of pleasant glee,
On a cloud I saw a child,
And he laughing said to me:

'Pipe a song about a Lamb!'
So I piped with merry cheer.
'Piper, pipe that song again.'
So I piped: he wept to hear.

'Drop thy pipe, thy happy pipe;
Sing thy songs of happy cheer!'
So I sung the same again,
While he wept with joy to hear.

'Piper, sit thee down and write
In a book, that all may read.'
So he vanished from my sight;
And I plucked a hollow reed,

And I made a rural pen,
And I stained the water clear,
And I wrote my happy songs
Every child may joy to hear.

The Fox and the Pheasants
An Aesop's Fable

One moonlight evening as Master Fox was taking his usual stroll in the woods, he saw a number of Pheasants perched quite out of his reach on a limb of a tall old tree. The sly Fox soon found a bright patch of moonlight, where the Pheasants could see him clearly; there he raised himself up on his hind legs, and began a wild dance. First he whirled 'round and 'round like a top, then he hopped up and down, cutting all sorts of strange capers. The Pheasants stared giddily. They hardly dared blink for fear of losing him out of their sight a single instant.

Now the Fox made as if to climb a tree, now he fell over and lay still, playing dead, and the next instant he was hopping on all fours, his back in the air, and his bushy tail shaking so that it seemed to throw out silver sparks in the moonlight.

By this time the poor birds' heads were in a whirl. And when the Fox began his performance all over again, so dazed did they become, that they lost their hold on the limb, and fell down one by one to the Fox.

Too much attention to danger may cause us to fall victims to it.

Exercise

In your workbook, underline all of the nouns that name people and places from this passage:

> So she told him all about Kansas, and how gray everything was there, and how the cyclone had carried her to this queer Land of Oz.

Which nouns are common and which are proper?

Copywork

Literature

So she told him all about Kansas and how the cyclone had carried her to this queer Land of Oz.

Poetry— Clouds

When the wind blows
You walk away slow,
White sheep, white sheep,
Where do you go?

5. Noun: Thing

- The Wonderful Wizard of Oz, Chapter 5

A noun is the name of a person, place, thing, or idea.

So far, you've learned about nouns that name people and nouns that name places. Today, we're going to talk about nouns that name things.

Everything has a name, and those names are nouns. Look around the room you are in and name some of the things you see. Is there a **table**, a **couch**, a **bookshelf**? All of these words are common nouns.

Things can also have proper names. We've been reading a book. **Book** is a common noun that doesn't refer to any one, specific book. The book we've been reading is entitled *The Wonderful Wizard of Oz*. The title of a book is a special, proper name.

Your toys are all things. The word **toys** is a common noun because it can refer to many different things. Do any of your toys have a special, proper name?

When we talk about things, this can also include living things like plants and animals. Dorothy has a pet dog. **Dog** is a common noun, and the proper name of Dorothy's dog is Toto!

What about the Scarecrow and the Tin Woodman? Are they people or living things? L. Frank Baum, the man who wrote this story, used nouns that are usually common nouns as their proper names! There can be many scarecrows, but there is only one named Scarecrow who talks and is friends with Dorothy.

Rain
by Robert Louis Stevenson

The rain is raining all around,
It falls on field and tree,
It rains on the umbrellas here,
And on the ships at sea.

The Dog in the Manger
An Aesop's Fable

A Dog asleep in a manger filled with hay, was awakened by the Cattle, which came in tired and hungry from working in the field. But the Dog would not let them get near the manger, and snarled and snapped as if it were filled with the best of meat and bones, all for himself.

The Cattle looked at the Dog in disgust. "How selfish he is!" said one. "He cannot eat the hay and yet he will not let us eat it who are so hungry for it!"

Now the farmer came in. When he saw how the Dog was acting, he seized a stick and drove him out of the stable with many a blow for his selfish behavior.

Do not grudge others what you cannot enjoy yourself.

Exercise

In your workbook, underline all of the nouns that name people, places, and things from this passage:

> The Tin Woodman gave a sigh of satisfaction and lowered his axe, which he leaned against the tree.

Which nouns are common and which are proper?

Copywork

Literature

> The Tin Woodman gave a sigh of satisfaction and lowered his axe, which he leaned against the tree.

Maxim

> Think before you speak.

6. Narration: The Young Crab and His Mother

- **The Wonderful Wizard of Oz, Chapter 6**

In this lesson, there is another fable written long ago by a man named Aesop. A fable is a story with a moral. Do you know what a moral is? A moral teaches a lesson about how we should act.

Today, you're going to do a narration. Your instructor will read this fable to you, and you will tell the story back to her while she writes it down for you. Then your instructor will write part of it for you to use as copywork.

Like L. Frank Baum in *The Wonderful Wizard of Oz*, Aesop uses nouns that are normally common nouns as special, proper names. Notice how Mother Crab and the little Crab both start with capital letters.

The Young Crab and His Mother
An Aesop's Fable

"Why in the world do you walk sideways like that?" said a Mother Crab to her son. "You should always walk straight forward with your toes turned out."

"Show me how to walk, mother dear," answered the little Crab obediently, "I want to learn."

So the old Crab tried and tried to walk straight forward. But she could walk sideways only, like her son. And when she wanted to turn her toes out she tripped and fell on her nose.

Do not tell others how to act unless you can set a good example.

Copywork

Narration

Instructor: Write or print part of today's narration to use as copywork.

Over in the Meadow
by Olive Wadsworth

Over in the meadow,
In the sand in the sun
Lived an old mother toadie
And her little toadie one.
"Wink!" said the mother;
"I wink!" said the one,
So they winked and they blinked
In the sand in the sun.

Over in the meadow,
Where the stream runs blue
Lived an old mother fish
And her little fishes two.
"Swim!" said the mother;
"We swim!" said the two,
So they swam and they leaped
Where the stream runs blue.

Over in the meadow,
In a hole in a tree
Lived an old mother bluebird
And her little birdies three.
"Sing!" said the mother;
"We sing!" said the three,
So they sang and were glad
In a hole in the tree.

Over in the meadow,
In the reeds on the shore
Lived an old mother muskrat
And her little ratties four.
"Dive!" said the mother;
"We dive!" said the four,
So they dived and they burrowed
In the reeds on the shore.

Over in the meadow,
In a snug beehive
Lived a mother honey bee
And her little bees five.
"Buzz!" said the mother;
"We buzz!" said the five,
So they buzzed and they hummed
In the snug beehive.

Over in the meadow,
In a nest built of sticks
Lived a black mother crow
And her little crows six.
"Caw!" said the mother;
"We caw!" said the six,
So they cawed and they called
In their nest built of sticks.

Over in the meadow,
Where the grass is so even
Lived a gay mother cricket
And her little crickets seven.
"Chirp!" said the mother;
"We chirp!" said the seven,
So they chirped cheery notes
In the grass soft and even.

Over in the meadow,
By the old mossy gate
Lived a brown mother lizard
And her little lizards eight.
"Bask!" said the mother;
"We bask!" said the eight,
So they basked in the sun
On the old mossy gate.

Over in the meadow,
Where the quiet pools shine
Lived a green mother frog
And her little froggies nine.
"Croak!" said the mother;
"We croak!" said the nine,
So they croaked and they splashed
Where the quiet pools shine.

Over in the meadow,
In a sly little den
Lived a gray mother spider
And her little spiders ten.
"Spin!" said the mother;
"We spin!" said the ten,
So they spun lacy webs
In their sly little den.

7. The Months of the Year

- The Wonderful Wizard of Oz, Chapter 7

The months of the year are January, February, March, April, May, June, July, August, September, October, November, and December.

Your new poem to copy is called "The Months" by Sara Coleridge. A year has twelve months. Each month brings new events, changes in the weather, and holidays! The poem tells us about things we can expect in each month, when certain flowers bloom, when it will be hot outside, and when the snow will come.

If you begin to keep a journal or a notebook, you can write down things that happen around your own home during the year. You can keep a record of when you first see various species of birds so that you'll know when to look for them the following year. A weather journal would tell you in which month it rains the most, and when to expect snow. You could also write down the birthdays of everyone in your home and which holidays your family celebrates.

Do you know your birthday? Your birthday is the month and day on which you were born.

Even if you're memorizing "The Months" by Sara Coleridge, you still need to memorize the months of the year in order. The names of the months are proper nouns, so they always start with a capital letter. Practice reading this list three times a day until you can say it without looking.

The Months
by Sara Coleridge

January brings the snow,
Makes our feet and fingers glow.

February brings the rain,
Thaws the frozen lake again.

March brings breezes loud and shrill,
Stirs the dancing daffodil.

April brings the primrose sweet,
Scatters daisies at our feet.

May brings flocks of pretty lambs,
Skipping by their fleecy dams.

June brings tulips, lilies, roses,
Fills the children's hand with posies.

Hot July brings cooling showers,
Apricots and gilliflowers.

August brings the sheaves of corn,
Then the harvest home is borne.

Warm September brings the fruit,
Sportsmen then begin to shoot.

Fresh October brings the pheasants,
Then to gather nuts is pleasant.

Dull November brings the blast,
Then the leaves are whirling fast.

Chill December brings the sleet,
Blazing fire, and Christmas treat.

The Stag and His Reflection
An Aesop's Fable

    A Stag, drinking from a crystal spring, saw himself mirrored in the clear water. He greatly admired the graceful arch of his antlers, but he was very much ashamed of his spindling legs.
    "How can it be," he sighed, "that I should be cursed with such legs when I have so magnificent a crown."
    At that moment he scented a panther and in an instant was bounding away through the forest. But as he ran his wide-spreading antlers caught in the branches of the trees, and soon the Panther overtook him. Then the Stag perceived that the legs of which he was so ashamed would have saved him had it not been for the useless ornaments on his head.
    We often make much of the ornamental and despise the useful.

Exercise

In your workbook, write N above each of the nouns from this passage. If a proper noun has more than one word, make arms stretched out to include the whole thing, like this: ———N———

> The Tin Woodman chopped a great pile of wood with his axe and Dorothy built a splendid fire that warmed her and made her feel less lonely.

Copywork

Literature

> Dorothy built a splendid fire that warmed her and made her feel less lonely.

Poetry—The Months

> January brings the snow,
> Makes our feet and fingers glow.
>
> February brings the rain,
> Thaws the frozen lake again.

8. Noun: Idea

- The Wonderful Wizard of Oz, Chapter 8

A noun is the name of a person, place, thing, or idea.

So far, you've learned about nouns that are the names of people, places, and things. People, places, and things all have a physical presence. They are real and solid. We can see, hear, smell, taste, or touch all of these.

The names of ideas are also nouns, but we can't reach out and touch ideas. We can't see, hear, taste, or smell them. But we can think about them and understand them.

Some ideas are our emotions, how we feel. Have you ever felt anger or sadness? **Anger** and **sadness** are both ideas, so their names are nouns. **Love** and **hope** can also be nouns. Can you think of others?

Not all ideas are about our emotions. Other ideas are freedom, peace, and kindness. Even though we can't see them or touch them, they're real and we can think about them.

The Chimney Sweeper
by William Blake

When my mother died I was very young,
And my father sold me while yet my tongue
Could scarcely cry 'Weep! weep! weep! weep!'
So your chimneys I sweep, and in soot I sleep.

There's little Tom Dacre, who cried when his head,
That curled like a lamb's back, was shaved; so I said,
'Hush, Tom! never mind it, for, when your head's bare,
You know that the soot cannot spoil your white hair.'

And so he was quiet, and that very night,
As Tom was a-sleeping, he had such a sight! —
That thousands of sweepers, Dick, Joe, Ned, and Jack,
Were all of them locked up in coffins of black.

And by came an angel, who had a bright key,
And he opened the coffins, and set them all free;
Then down a green plain, leaping, laughing, they run
And wash in a river, and shine in the sun.

Then naked and white, all their bags left behind,
They rise upon clouds, and sport in the wind:
And the angel told Tom, if he'd be a good boy,
He'd have God for his father, and never want joy.

And so Tom awoke, and we rose in the dark,
And got with our bags and our brushes to work.
Though the morning was cold, Tom was happy and warm:
So, if all do their duty, they need not fear harm.

The Wolf and the Ass
An Aesop's Fable

An Ass was feeding in a pasture near a wood when he saw a Wolf lurking in the shadows along the hedge. He easily guessed what the Wolf had in mind, and thought of a plan to save himself. So he pretended he was lame, and began to hobble painfully.

When the Wolf came up, he asked the Ass what had made him lame, and the Ass replied that he had stepped on a sharp thorn.

"Please pull it out," he pleaded, groaning as if in pain. "If you do not, it might stick in your throat when you eat me."

The Wolf saw the wisdom of the advice, for he wanted to enjoy his meal without any danger of choking. So the Ass lifted up his foot and the Wolf began to search very closely and carefully for the thorn.

Just then the Ass kicked out with all his might, tumbling the Wolf a dozen paces away. And while the Wolf was getting very slowly and painfully to his feet, the Ass galloped away in safety.

"Serves me right," growled the Wolf as he crept into the bushes. "I'm a butcher by trade, not a doctor."

Stick to your trade.

Exercise

In your workbook, write N above each of the nouns from this passage:

> It was a lovely country, with plenty of flowers and fruit trees and sunshine to cheer them, and had they not felt so sorry for the poor Scarecrow, they could have been very happy.

Copywork

Literature

It was a lovely country, with plenty of flowers and fruit trees and sunshine to cheer them.

Bible—Philippians 4:13

I can do all things through Him who strengthens me.

Peasants Bringing Home a Calf Born in the Fields by Jean-Francois Millet

Picture Study

1. Read the title and the name of the artist. Study the picture for several minutes, then put the picture away.

2. Describe the picture.

3. Look at the picture again. Do you notice any details that you missed before? What do you like or dislike about this painting? Does it remind you of anything?

9. Quotations; Picture Study: Peasants Bringing Home a Calf Born in the Fields

- The Wonderful Wizard of Oz, Chapter 9

We use punctuation marks to make it easier to read. We end sentences with a punctuation mark to let us know the sentence has ended. The three punctuation marks that end sentences are the period (.), the question mark (?), and the exclamation mark (!). Each one tells us something about the type of sentence.

Sometimes we want to write down exactly what someone has said. When we write down exactly what someone has said, this is called a **direct quotation**. When we do this, we need a special type of punctuation mark called a **quotation mark**. Look at this sentence from chapter eight of *The Wonderful Wizard of Oz*.

"If we leave her here she will die," said the Lion.

Part of this sentence is exactly what the Lion said, so we wrap that part in quotation marks by putting them at the beginning and at the end of the direct quotation. The Lion did not say **said the Lion**, so we do not put that part inside the quotation marks. That part is there to tell the reader who said this direct quotation. We use the comma (,) to separate the direct quotation from the rest of the sentence. The comma comes before the ending quotation mark.

There's another way we can say that sentence without using the Lion's exact words:

The Lion said that if they left her there she would die.

Here, we've reported what the Lion said, but we did not use his exact words. This sentence is an **indirect quotation**. Since we did not use the Lion's exact words, we do not need quotation marks.

Some One
by Walter de la Mare

Some one came knocking
   At my wee, small door;
Some one came knocking,
   I'm sure—sure—sure;

I listened, I opened,
   I looked to left and right,
But naught there was a-stirring
   In the still dark night;
Only the busy beetle
   Tap-tapping in the wall,
Only from the forest
   The screech-owl's call,
Only the cricket whistling
   While the dewdrops fall,
So I know not who came knocking,
At all, at all, at all.

Exercise

In your workbook, write N above each of the nouns from this passage:

> "We cannot be far from the road of yellow brick, now," remarked the Scarecrow, as he stood beside the girl, "for we have come nearly as far as the river carried us away."

Can you change the direct quotation to an indirect quotation?

Copywork

Literature

> "We cannot be far from the road of yellow brick, now," remarked the Scarecrow.

10. Name and Initials

- The Wonderful Wizard of Oz, Chapter 10

Most people have three names. Your first name is the name that most people call you unless you have a nickname. A nickname is usually a shorter form of someone's first name, like Dan or Danny for Daniel or Jenny for Jennifer. What is your first name?

Your middle name comes between your first name and your last name. Your mother may call you by both your first and middle names when she wants to get your attention. What is your middle name?

Your last name is also called a family name because you have the same last name as your father or mother. Often, a whole family has the same last name because your mother may have changed her last name to be the same as your father's when they got married.

What is your full name: first, middle, and last? What are the full names of the members of your family? Your name is a proper noun, so always begin it with a capital letter.

Sometimes, you might need to write your initials instead of your full name. **Initial** means first. When we write our initials, we write only the first letter of all three of our names. We capitalize each letter and put a period after it. Here's how I write my initials:

K. J. D.

Singing
by Robert Louis Stevenson

Of speckled eggs the birdie sings
    And nests among the trees;
The sailor sings of ropes and things
    In ships upon the seas.

The children sing in far Japan,
    The children sing in Spain;
The organ with the organ man
    Is singing in the rain.

The Wolf and the House Dog
An Aesop's Fable

There was once a Wolf who got very little to eat because the Dogs of the village were so wide awake and watchful. He was really nothing but skin and bones, and it made him very downhearted to think of it.

One night this Wolf happened to fall in with a fine fat House Dog who had wandered a little too far from home. The Wolf would gladly have eaten him then and there, but the House Dog looked strong enough to leave his marks should he try it. So the Wolf spoke very humbly to the Dog, complimenting him on his fine appearance.

"You can be as well-fed as I am if you want to," replied the Dog. "Leave the woods; there you live miserably. Why, you have to fight hard for every bite you get. Follow my example and you will get along beautifully."

"What must I do?" asked the Wolf.

"Hardly anything," answered the House Dog. "Chase people who carry canes, bark at beggars, and fawn on the people of the house. In return you will get tidbits of every kind, bones, choice bits of meat, sugar, cake, and much more beside, not to speak of kind words and caresses."

The Wolf had such a beautiful vision of his coming happiness that he almost wept. But just then he noticed that the hair on the Dog's neck was worn and the skin was chafed.

"What is that on your neck?"

"Nothing at all," replied the Dog.

"What! nothing!"

"Oh, just a trifle!"

"But please tell me."

"Perhaps you see the mark of the collar to which my chain is fastened."

"What! A chain!" cried the Wolf. "Don't you go wherever you please?"

"Not always! But what's the difference?" replied the Dog.

"All the difference in the world! I don't care a rap for your feasts and I wouldn't take all the tender young lambs in the world at that price." And away ran the Wolf to the woods.

There is nothing worth so much as liberty.

Exercise

In your workbook, write N above each of the nouns from this passage. If a proper noun has more than one word, make arms stretched out to include the whole thing, like this: ———N———

> It was some time before the Cowardly Lion awakened, for he had lain among the poppies a long while, breathing in their deadly fragrance.

Which nouns are common and which are proper?

Copywork

Literature

Today, ask your instructor to write your name and your initials for you to copy in your workbook. If you want, there's room to write the names or initials of some of your family members as well.

Poetry—The Months

March brings breezes loud and shrill,
Stirs the dancing daffodil.

April brings the primrose sweet,
Scatters daisies at our feet.

11. Definition: Verb: Action Verb

- The Wonderful Wizard of Oz, Chapter 11

A verb is a word that shows action or state of being.

A noun is the name of name a person, place, thing, or idea. When we talk about nouns, we want to know what the person, place, thing, or idea is doing. A verb is a word that shows action. Verbs show what nouns do.

Can you think of some actions, things you like to do? Maybe you like to **run** and **play** outside. **Stand** up for a moment and **show** some action. Can you **hop**? **Skip**? **Jump**? Do you **read** this book, or do you **listen** while someone **reads** it to you?

Do you have brothers or sisters? What are they doing right now?

In *The Wonderful Wizard of Oz,* Dorothy and her friends **travel** to the Emerald City. They **walk** along the road of yellow brick. Sometimes, they **stop** and **talk** with people. They **eat** and **drink** and **sleep**.

All of the bold words are verbs. They express action and tell us what nouns are doing. If a word is something you can do, it is an action verb.

The Moon's the North Wind's Cooky
by Vachel Lindsay

The Moon's the North Wind's cooky.
He bites it, day by day,
Until there's but a rim of scraps
That crumble all away.

The South Wind is a baker.
He kneads clouds in his den,
And bakes a crisp new moon that . . . greedy
North . . . Wind . . . eats . . . again!

A Raven and a Swan
An Aesop's Fable

A Raven, which you know is black as coal, was envious of the Swan, because her feathers were as white as the purest snow. The foolish bird got the idea that if he lived like the Swan, swimming and diving all day long and eating the weeds and plants that grow in the water, his feathers would turn white like the Swan's.

So he left his home in the woods and fields and flew down to live on the lakes and in the marshes. But though he washed and washed all day long, almost drowning himself at it, his feathers remained as black as ever. And as the water weeds he ate did not agree with him, he got thinner and thinner, and at last he died.

A change of habits will not alter nature.

Exercise

In your workbook, write V above each of the verbs from this passage:

> "But I spoke to him as he sat behind his screen and gave him your message. He said he will grant you an audience, if you so desire."

[Note to instructor: There is one helping verb in the second sentence. It's fine if the child recognizes it as a verb, but not necessary. The purpose of this exercise is only to find the six action verbs.]

Copywork

Literature

> "But I spoke to him as he sat behind his screen and gave him your message."

Maxim

> Honesty is the best policy.

12. Narration: The Boy and the Filberts

- The Wonderful Wizard of Oz, Chapter 12

It's time for a narration. Your instructor will read this fable to you, and you will tell the story back to her while she writes it down for you. Then your instructor will write part of it for you to use as copywork.

The Boy and the Filberts
An Aesop's Fable

A Boy was given permission to put his hand into a pitcher to get some filberts. But he took such a great fistful that he could not draw his hand out again. There he stood, unwilling to give up a single filbert and yet unable to get them all out at once. Vexed and disappointed, he began to cry.

"My boy," said his mother, "be satisfied with half the nuts you have taken and you will easily get your hand out. Then perhaps you may have some more filberts some other time."

Do not attempt too much at once.

The Bumblebee
by James Whitcomb Riley

You better not fool with a Bumblebee! —
Ef you don't think they can sting — you'll see!
They're lazy to look at, an' kind o' go
Buzzin' an' bummin' aroun' so slow,
An' ac' so slouchy an' all fagged out,
Danglin' their legs as they drone about
The hollyhawks 'at they can't climb in
'Ithout ist a-tumble-un out ag'in!
Wunst I watched one climb clean 'way
In a jimson-blossom, I did, one day, —
An' I ist grabbed it — an' nen let go —
An' "Ooh-ooh! Honey! I told ye so!"
Says The Raggedy Man; an' he ist run

An' pullt out the stinger, an' don't laugh none,
An' says: "They has be'n folks, I guess,
'At thought I wuz predjudust, more er less, —
Yit I still muntain 'at a Bumblebee
Wears out his welcome too quick fer me!"

Copywork

Narration

Instructor: Write or print part of today's narration to use as copywork.

13. Writing Dates

- The Wonderful Wizard of Oz, Chapter 13

> The months of the year are January, February, March, April, May, June, July, August, September, October, November, and December.

Thirty Days Hath September
A Mother Goose Rhyme

Thirty days hath September,
April, June and November,
All the rest have thirty-one,
Excepting February alone,
Which has but twenty-eight days clear
And twenty-nine in each leap year.

There are twelve months in the year, and each month has a specific number of days in it. Memorize the Mother Goose rhyme "Thirty Days Hath September" to help you remember how many days are in each month. The poem reminds us that September, April, June, and November all have thirty days. All of the other months have thirty-one days, except for one: February. February alone has only twenty-eight days, except in leap year.

What is leap year? Normally, our year has 365 days, but every four years is a leap year when the year has 366 days. We add the extra day to the end of February, so in leap years, February has twenty-nine days.

When we write the date, we include the month, the day, and the year. Every year has a January 1, a December 31, and everything in between. We have to include the year or else we won't know if something happened this year or thirty years ago. When we write the date, we put a comma between the day and the year like this:

July 20, 2008

When is your birthday? In what year were you born? Every year, you'll have a birthday, but knowing the year in which you were born tells us how old you are.

The Mouse and the Weasel
An Aesop's Fable

A little hungry Mouse found his way one day into a basket of corn. He had to squeeze himself a good deal to get through the narrow opening between the strips of the basket. But the corn was tempting and the Mouse was determined to get in. When at last he had succeeded, he gorged himself to bursting. Indeed he became about three times as big around the middle as he was when he went in.

At last he felt satisfied and dragged himself to the opening to get out again. But the best he could do was to get his head out. So there he sat groaning and moaning, both from the discomfort inside him and his anxiety to escape from the basket.

Just then a Weasel came by. He understood the situation quickly.

"My friend," he said, "I know what you've been doing. You've been stuffing. That's what you get. You will have to stay there till you feel just like you did when you went in. Good night, and good enough for you."

And that was all the sympathy the poor Mouse got.

Greediness leads to misfortune.

Exercise

In your workbook, write V above each of the verbs from this passage:

> So they called the yellow Winkies and asked them if they would help to rescue their friends, and the Winkies said that they would be delighted to do all in their power for Dorothy, who had set them free from bondage.

Can you change the indirect quotations to direct quotations? You'll have to make up the exact words said.

Copywork

Literature

Ask your instructor to write today's date and your birthday for you to copy in your workbook. If you want, there's room to write the birthdays of some of your family members as well, or you can practice writing your name again.

Poetry—The Months

May brings flocks of pretty lambs,
Skipping by their fleecy dams.

June brings tulips, lilies, roses,
Fills the children's hand with posies.

14. Quotations

- The Wonderful Wizard of Oz, Chapter 14

Remember that direct quotations tell us the exact words that someone spoke. We use quotation marks to separate the exact words spoken from the rest of the sentence. Indirect quotations report what someone has said, but without using the exact words spoken. Look at the following sentence from *The Wonderful Wizard of Oz*. Is this a direct quotation or an indirect quotation?

> "If we walk far enough," said Dorothy, "I am sure we shall sometime come to some place."

The sentence above is a direct quotation. These are the exact words that Dorothy spoke. Can you change that sentence to an indirect quotation? Here's one way:

> Dorothy said that she was sure if they walked far enough, they would sometime get to some place.

Look at the following sentences. Are these indirect quotations or direct quotations?

> The next day they called the Winkies together and bade them good-bye.

> The Winkies were sorry to have them go, and they had grown so fond of the Tin Woodman that they begged him to stay and rule over them and the Yellow Land of the West.

Can you change the above sentences to direct quotations? You don't know the exact words they said, so you'll have to make them up!

Which is the Favorite?
by Charles Lamb

Brothers and sisters I have many:
Though I know there is not any
Of them but I love, yet I
Will just name them all; and try

If there be one a little more
Loved by me than all the rest.
Yes; I do think, that I love best
My brother Henry, because he
Has always been most fond of me.
Yet, to be sure, there's Isabel;
I think I love her quite as well.
And, I assure you, little Ann,
No brother nor no sister can
Be more dear to me than she.
Only I must say, Emily,
Being the eldest, it's right her
To all the rest I should prefer.
Yet after all I've said, suppose
My greatest favorite should be Rose.
No, John and Paul are both more dear
To me than Rose, that's always here,
While they are half the year at school;
And yet that neither is no rule.
I've named them all, there's only seven;
I find my love to all so even,
To every sister, every brother,
I love not one more than another.

The Wolf and the Lean Dog
An Aesop's Fable

A Wolf prowling near a village one evening met a Dog. It happened to be a very lean and bony Dog, and Master Wolf would have turned up his nose at such meager fare had he not been more hungry than usual. So he began to edge toward the Dog, while the Dog backed away.

"Let me remind your lordship," said the Dog, his words interrupted now and then as he dodged a snap of the Wolf's teeth, "how unpleasant it would be to eat me now. Look at my ribs. I am nothing but skin and bone. But let me tell you something in private. In a few days my master will give a wedding feast for his only daughter. You can guess how fine and fat I will grow on the scraps from the table. Then is the time to eat me."

The Wolf could not help thinking how nice it would be to have a fine fat Dog to eat instead of the scrawny object before him. So he went away pulling in his belt and promising to return.

Some days later the Wolf came back for the promised feast. He found the Dog in his master's yard, and asked him to come out and be eaten.

"Sir," said the Dog, with a grin, "I shall be delighted to have you eat me. I'll be out as soon as the porter opens the door."

But the "porter" was a huge Dog whom the Wolf knew by painful experience to be very unkind toward wolves. So he decided not to wait and made off as fast as his legs could carry him.

Do not depend on the promises of those whose interest it is to deceive you.

Take what you can get when you can get it.

Exercise

In your workbook, write V above each of the verbs from this passage:

> "Suppose we call the field mice," she suggested. "They could probably tell us the way to the Emerald City."

Can you change the direct quotation to an indirect quotation?

Copywork

Literature

> "Suppose we call the field mice," she suggested. "They could probably tell us the way to the Emerald City."

Bible—Hebrews 13:8

> Jesus Christ is the same yesterday and today and forever.

The Knitting Lesson by Jean-Francois Millet

Picture Study

1. Read the title and the name of the artist. Study the picture for several minutes, then put the picture away.

2. Describe the picture.

3. Look at the picture again. Do you notice any details that you missed before? What do you like or dislike about this painting? Does it remind you of anything?

15. Invisible Action Verbs; Picture Study: The Knitting Lesson

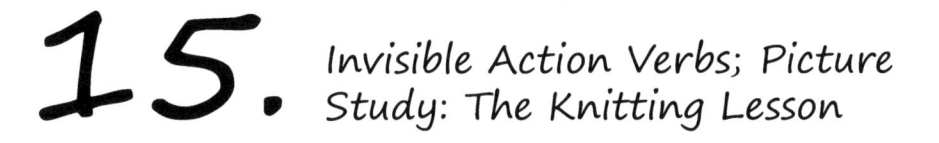

- The Wonderful Wizard of Oz, Chapter 15

A verb is a word that shows action or state of being.

A verb is a word that shows action.

Can you **touch** your nose? Can you **walk** around the room? Can you **eat** your dinner? All of the bold words are action verbs. They tell us what you do. If you can do something, it is an action verb.

Usually, we can **observe** action verbs. I can **see** a bird **fly**. I can **hear** a dog **bark**. If a bug **touches** me, I can **feel** it. If something **burns**, I can **smell** it.

There are some action verbs that we can't observe. We can't see it when someone **thinks**, or when someone **knows** something, or when someone **dreams**. These are all still action verbs. We can do these things, but others can't observe the action. Can you think of any other invisible action verbs?

[Instructor: If necessary, prompt the child for invisible action verbs like hope, pray, love.]

Make sentences from the following nouns by supplying an action verb:

The baby _____.

The cat _____.

Cows _____.

My mother _____.

My father _____.

Birds _____.

Tigers _____.

The bookshelf _____.

Dream Song
by Walter de la Mare

    Sunlight, moonlight,
    Twilight, starlight-
Gloaming at the close of day,
    And an owl calling,
    Cool dews falling
In a wood of oak and may.

    Lantern-light, taper-light,
    Torchlight, no-light:
Darkness at the shut of day,
    And lions roaring,
    Their wrath pouring
In wild waste places far away.

    Elf-light, bat-light,
    Touchwood-light and toad-light,
And the sea a shimmering gloom of grey,
    And a small face smiling
    In a dream's beguiling
In a world of wonders far away.

Exercise

In your workbook, write V above each of the verbs from this passage:

> "Then I thought, as the country was so green and beautiful, I would call it the Emerald City"

Don't miss the invisible action verb!

Copywork

Literature

> "Then I thought, as the country was so green and beautiful, I would call it the Emerald City"

16. Definition: Pronoun

- The Wonderful Wizard of Oz, Chapter 16

A pronoun is a word used in the place of a noun.

Look at these sentences:

> Next morning the Scarecrow said to <u>the Scarecrow's</u> friends: "Congratulate <u>the Scarecrow</u>. <u>The Scarecrow</u> is going to Oz to get <u>the Scarecrow's</u> brains at last. When <u>the Scarecrow</u> returns <u>the Scarecrow</u> shall be as other men are."

That's how *The Wonderful Wizard of Oz* would read if we didn't have a special type of word called a pronoun. A pronoun is a word used in the place of a noun. We use pronouns because the sentences above are hard to say, hard to write, and hard to understand! See the difference when we put the pronouns back into these sentences:

> Next morning the Scarecrow said to <u>his</u> friends: "Congratulate <u>me</u>. <u>I</u> am going to Oz to get <u>my</u> brains at last. When <u>I</u> return <u>I</u> shall be as other men are."

The underlined words are pronouns. Isn't that much better?

Every pronoun has an antecedent. An antecedent is the noun that a pronoun replaces in a sentence. In the sentences above, all of the pronouns are replacing **the Scarecrow**, so **the Scarecrow** is the antecedent for each pronoun.

On the Bridge
by Kate Greenaway

If I could see a little fish—
That is what I just now wish!
I want to see his great round eyes
Always open in surprise.

I wish a water-rat would glide
Slowly to the other side;

Or a dancing spider sit
On the yellow flags a bit.

I think I'll get some stones to throw,
And watch the pretty circles show.
Or shall we sail a flower boat,
And watch it slowly—slowly float?

That's nice—because you never know
How far away it means to go;
And when tomorrow comes, you see,
It may be in the great wide sea.

The Cock and the Fox
An Aesop's Fable

One bright evening as the sun was sinking on a glorious world a wise old Cock flew into a tree to roost. Before he composed himself to rest, he flapped his wings three times and crowed loudly. But just as he was about to put his head under his wing, his beady eyes caught a flash of red and a glimpse of a long pointed nose, and there just below him stood Master Fox.

"Have you heard the wonderful news?" cried the Fox in a very joyful and excited manner.

"What news?" asked the Cock very calmly. But he had a queer, fluttery feeling inside him, for, you know, he was very much afraid of the Fox.

"Your family and mine and all other animals have agreed to forget their differences and live in peace and friendship from now on forever. Just think of it! I simply cannot wait to embrace you! Do come down, dear friend, and let us celebrate the joyful event."

"How grand!" said the Cock. "I certainly am delighted at the news." But he spoke in an absent way, and stretching up on tiptoes, seemed to be looking at something afar off.

"What is it you see?" asked the Fox a little anxiously.

"Why, it looks to me like a couple of Dogs coming this way. They must have heard the good news and—"

But the Fox did not wait to hear more. Off he started on a run.

"Wait," cried the Cock. "Why do you run? The Dogs are friends of yours now!"

"Yes," answered the Fox. "But they might not have heard the news. Besides, I have a very important errand that I had almost forgotten about."

The Cock smiled as he buried his head in his feathers and went to sleep, for he had succeeded in outwitting a very crafty enemy.

The trickster is easily tricked.

Exercise

In your workbook, first write N above each of the nouns and then write V above each of the verbs from this passage. If a proper noun has more than one word, make arms stretched out to include the whole thing, like this: ———N———

Then he said good-bye to them all in a cheerful voice and went to the Throne Room, where he rapped upon the door.

Copywork

Literature

Then he said good-bye to them all in a cheerful voice and went to the Throne Room

Poetry—The Months

Hot July brings cooling showers,
Apricots and gilliflowers.

August brings the sheaves of corn,
Then the harvest home is borne.

17. First Person Pronouns

- The Wonderful Wizard of Oz, Chapter 17

A pronoun is a word used in the place of a noun.

Do you know what the words singular and plural mean? Singular means only one, like the word single. Plural means more than one. We use different pronouns depending on whether the noun we're replacing is singular, only one, or plural, more than one.

First person pronouns are used when someone is speaking of himself. The first person singular pronouns are: I, me, my, mine. Look at these sentences from *The Wonderful Wizard of Oz*. The first person singular pronouns are underlined.

"How can I cross the desert?" she inquired.

"We!" exclaimed the girl. "Are you going with me?"

"Now, it is quite beyond my powers to make a cyclone."

"If your heads were stuffed with straw, like mine, you would probably all live in the beautiful places."

The first person plural pronouns are: we, us, our, ours. In the following sentences from *The Wonderful Wizard of Oz*, the first person plural pronouns are underlined.

"We will begin to work on our balloon."

"If it won't float," remarked Dorothy, "it will be of no use to us."

Dorothy could also say:

"This balloon is ours."

Good Night! Good Night!
by Victor Hugo

Good night! Good night!
Far flies the light;
But still God's love
Shall flame above,
Making all bright.
Good night! Good night!

The Dog and His Reflection
An Aesop's Fable

    A Dog, to whom the butcher had thrown a bone, was hurrying home with his prize as fast as he could go. As he crossed a narrow footbridge, he happened to look down and saw himself reflected in the quiet water as if in a mirror. But the greedy Dog thought he saw a real Dog carrying a bone much bigger than his own.

    If he had stopped to think he would have known better. But instead of thinking, he dropped his bone and sprang at the Dog in the river, only to find himself swimming for dear life to reach the shore. At last he managed to scramble out, and as he stood sadly thinking about the good bone he had lost, he realized what a stupid Dog he had been.

    It is very foolish to be greedy.

Exercise

In your workbook, underline the first person pronouns from this passage:

> "Thank you," he answered. "Now, if you will help me sew the silk together, we will begin to work on our balloon."

Copywork

Literature

> "Now, if you will help me sew the silk together, we will begin to work on our balloon."

Maxim

> A stitch in time saves nine.

18. Narration: The Crow and the Pitcher

- The Wonderful Wizard of Oz, Chapter 18

It's time for a narration. Your instructor will read this fable to you, and you will tell the story back to her while she writes it down for you. Then your instructor will write part of it for you to use as copywork.

The Crow and the Pitcher
An Aesop's Fable

In a spell of dry weather, when the Birds could find very little to drink, a thirsty Crow found a pitcher with a little water in it. But the pitcher was high and had a narrow neck, and no matter how he tried, the Crow could not reach the water. The poor thing felt as if he must die of thirst.

Then an idea came to him. Picking up some small pebbles, he dropped them into the pitcher one by one. With each pebble the water rose a little higher until at last it was near enough so he could drink.

In a pinch a good use of our wits may help us out.

Nicholas Nye
by Walter de la Mare

Thistle and darnell and dock grew there,
   And a bush, in the corner, of may,
On the orchard wall I used to sprawl
   In the blazing heat of the day;
Half asleep and half awake,
   While the birds went twittering by,
And nobody there my lone to share
   But Nicholas Nye.

Nicholas Nye was lean and gray,
   Lame of leg and old,
More than a score of donkey's years
   He had been since he was foaled;
He munched the thistles, purple and spiked,
   Would sometimes stoop and sigh,

And turn to his head, as if he said,
  "Poor Nicholas Nye!"

Alone with his shadow he'd drowse in the meadow,
  Lazily swinging his tail,
At break of day he used to bray,—
  Not much too hearty and hale;
But a wonderful gumption was under his skin,
  And a clean calm light in his eye,
And once in a while; he'd smile:—
  Would Nicholas Nye.

Seem to be smiling at me, he would,
  From his bush in the corner, of may,—
Bony and ownerless, widowed and worn,
  Knobble-kneed, lonely and gray;
And over the grass would seem to pass
  'Neath the deep dark blue of the sky,
Something much better than words between me
  And Nicholas Nye.

But dusk would come in the apple boughs,
  The green of the glow-worm shine,
The birds in nest would crouch to rest,
  And home I'd trudge to mine;
And there, in the moonlight, dark with dew,
  Asking not wherefore nor why,
Would brood like a ghost, and as still as a post,
  Old Nicholas Nye.

Copywork

Narration

> Instructor: Write or print part of today's narration to use as copywork.

19. First Person Pronouns

- The Wonderful Wizard of Oz, Chapter 19

A pronoun is a word used in the place of a noun.

Remember that first person pronouns are used when someone is speaking of himself, and singular means only one. The first person singular pronouns are: I, me, my, mine. Complete each of the following sentences using a first person singular pronoun.

_____ made a balloon.

The balloon is for _____.

This is _____ balloon.

This balloon is _____.

Remember that plural means more than one. The first person plural pronouns are: we, us, our, ours. Complete each of the following sentences using a first person plural pronoun.

_____ traveled to the Emerald City.

The Great Oz met with _____.

He listened to _____ requests.

The rewards are _____.

The Yak
by Hilaire Belloc

As a friend to the children
Commend me the Yak.
You will find it exactly the thing:
It will carry and fetch, you can ride on its back,
Or lead it about with a string.

The Tartar who dwells on the plains of Thibet
(A desolate region of snow)
Has for centuries made it a nursery pet,
And surely the Tartar should know!
Then tell your papa where the Yak can be got,
And if he is awfully rich
He will buy you the creature—
or else
  he will not.
(I cannot be positive which.)

The Lark and Her Young Ones
An Aesop's Fable

    A Lark made her nest in a field of young wheat. As the days passed, the wheat stalks grew tall and the young birds, too, grew in strength. Then one day, when the ripe golden grain waved in the breeze, the Farmer and his son came into the field.

    "This wheat is now ready for reaping," said the Farmer. "We must call in our neighbors and friends to help us harvest it."

    The young Larks in their nest close by were much frightened, for they knew they would be in great danger if they did not leave the nest before the reapers came. When the Mother Lark returned with food for them, they told her what they had heard.

    "Do not be frightened, children," said the Mother Lark. "If the Farmer said he would call in his neighbors and friends to help him do his work, this wheat will not be reaped for a while yet."

    A few days later, the wheat was so ripe, that when the wind shook the stalks, a hail of wheat grains came rustling down on the young Larks' heads.

    "If this wheat is not harvested at once," said the Farmer, "we shall lose half the crop. We cannot wait any longer for help from our friends. Tomorrow we must set to work, ourselves."

    When the young Larks told their mother what they had heard that day, she said:

    "Then we must be off at once. When a man decides to do his own work and not depend on any one else, then you may be sure there will be no more delay."

    There was much fluttering and trying out of wings that afternoon, and at sunrise next day, when the Farmer and his son cut down the grain, they found an empty nest.

    Self-help is the best help.

Exercise

In your workbook, underline the first person pronouns from this passage:

> As Dorothy bade the good-natured Guardian a last farewell she said: "I have been very kindly treated in your lovely City, and everyone has been good to me. I cannot tell you how grateful I am."

Do you remember what an antecedent is? An antecedent is the noun that has been replaced by a pronoun. What noun is replaced by the first person pronouns in these sentences?

Copywork

Literature

> "I have been very kindly treated in your lovely City, and everyone has been good to me."

Poetry—The Months

> Warm September brings the fruit,
> Sportsmen then begin to shoot.
>
> Fresh October brings the pheasants,
> Then to gather nuts is pleasant.

20. Abbreviations: Months, Streets

- The Wonderful Wizard of Oz, Chapter 20

Do you know what the word abbreviation means? It means brief!

Sometimes when we write words, we use an abbreviation instead of writing the entire word. When we use abbreviations for the months, we only write the first three letters of the name of the month. Look at the abbreviations below. What is at the end of each abbreviation?

January	Jan.	July	Jul.
February	Feb.	August	Aug.
March	Mar.	September	Sep.
April	Apr.	October	Oct.
May	May	November	Nov.
June	Jun.	December	Dec.

An abbreviation ends with a period. The names of the months are proper nouns, so each abbreviation begins with a capital letter just as the name of the month does. Why doesn't the abbreviation for May end with a period?

Sometimes, you may see **Sept.** as the abbreviation for September.

Here are some other common abbreviations that we use when naming streets and roads. What's the name of the street on which you live?

Street	St.	Boulevard	Bvd.
Road	Rd.	Circle	Cir.
Avenue	Ave.	Highway	Hwy.

Who Has Seen the Wind?
by Christina Rossetti

Who has seen the wind?
Neither I nor you:
But when the leaves hang trembling,
The wind is passing through.

Who has seen the wind?
Neither you nor I:
But when the trees bow down their heads,
The wind is passing by.

The Wolf and the Lamb
An Aesop's Fable

    A stray Lamb stood drinking early one morning on the bank of a woodland stream. That very same morning a hungry Wolf came by farther up the stream, hunting for something to eat. He soon got his eyes on the Lamb. As a rule Mr. Wolf snapped up such delicious morsels without making any bones about it, but this Lamb looked so very helpless and innocent that the Wolf felt he ought to have some kind of an excuse for taking its life.

    "How dare you paddle around in my stream and stir up all the mud!" he shouted fiercely. "You deserve to be punished severely for your rashness!"

    "But, your highness," replied the trembling Lamb, "do not be angry! I cannot possibly muddy the water you are drinking up there. Remember, you are upstream and I am downstream."

    "You do muddy it!" retorted the Wolf savagely. "And besides, I have heard that you told lies about me last year!"

    "How could I have done so?" pleaded the Lamb. "I wasn't born until this year."

    "If it wasn't you, it was your brother!"

    "I have no brothers."

    "Well, then," snarled the Wolf, "It was someone in your family anyway. But no matter who it was, I do not intend to be talked out of my breakfast."

    And without more words the Wolf seized the poor Lamb and carried her off to the forest.

    The tyrant can always find an excuse for his tyranny.

    The unjust will not listen to the reasoning of the innocent.

Exercise

In your workbook, write N above each of the nouns and V above each of the verbs from this passage:

> So the Scarecrow climbed farther up and sat down on the top of the wall, and Dorothy put her head over and cried, "Oh, my!" just as the Scarecrow had done.

Copywork

Abbreviations for Months

Jan.	Feb.	Mar.
Apr.	May	Jun.
Jul.	Aug.	Sep.
Oct.	Nov.	Dec.

Bible—Psalm 145:9

The Lord is good to all,
And His mercies are over all His works.

The Bouquet of Margueritas by Jean-Francois Millet

Picture Study

1. Read the title and the name of the artist. Study the picture for several minutes, then put the picture away.

2. Describe the picture.

3. Look at the picture again. Do you notice any details that you missed before? What do you like or dislike about this painting? Does it remind you of anything?

21. Capitalization; Picture Study: The Bouquet of Margueritas

- The Wonderful Wizard of Oz, Chapter 21

Think of some examples of when we capitalize words, then read the following list and examples.

- Capitalize proper nouns. George Washington, Chicago, Grand Canyon— these are all proper nouns, so we capitalize them.

- Capitalize the pronoun I. The pronoun I is always capitalized. Never write the pronoun I as a lower-case letter.

- Capitalize the first word in a sentence.

- Capitalize the first word of every line of a poem.

- Capitalize titles. *The Wonderful Wizard of Oz*— this is the title of a book, so we capitalize every word except for little ones like a, an, the, and, of, or. Only capitalize a little word in a title when it is the first word in the title. These rules are the same for the title of a poem.

Garden and Cradle
by Eugene Field

When our babe he goeth walking in his garden,
Around his tinkling feet the sunbeams play;
The posies they are good to him,
And bow them as they should to him,
As fareth he upon his kingly way;
And birdlings of the wood to him
Make music, gentle music, all the day,
When our babe he goeth walking in his garden.

When our babe he goeth swinging in his cradle,
Then the night it looketh ever sweetly down;
The little stars are kind to him,
The moon she hath a mind to him

And layeth on his head a golden crown;
And singeth then the wind to him
A song, the gentle song of Bethlem-town,
When our babe he goeth swinging in his cradle.

Exercise

In your workbook, underline the first person pronouns from this passage:

> "Not a bit of it," answered the Lion. "I should like to live here all my life. See how soft the dried leaves are under your feet and how rich and green the moss is that clings to these old trees."

Do you remember what an antecedent is? An antecedent is the noun that has been replaced by a pronoun. What noun is replaced by the first person pronouns in these sentences?

Copywork

Literature

> "Not a bit of it," answered the Lion. "I should like to live here all my life."

22. Second Person Pronouns

- The Wonderful Wizard of Oz, Chapter 22

A pronoun is a word used in the place of a noun.

Remember that first person pronouns are used when someone is speaking of himself. The first person pronouns are: I, me, my, mine, we, us, our, ours.

Today, we shall learn about the second person pronouns. Second person pronouns are used for the person to whom we are speaking. The second person pronouns are: you, your, yours. I might say to you:

"How are <u>you</u> today?"

"Is this <u>your</u> book?"

"Are these toys <u>yours</u>?"

Look at this sentence from *The Wonderful Wizard of Oz*. The second person pronouns are underlined.

"Now the Golden Cap is <u>yours</u>, and three times <u>you</u> have the right to lay <u>your</u> wishes upon us."

Here, the Monkey King is speaking to Dorothy, so he uses the second person pronouns you, your, and yours to replace Dorothy's name.

With the second person, the pronouns are the same for both singular, only one, and plural, more than one. In the following sentences from *The Wonderful Wizard of Oz*, the Lion is speaking to all the beasts in the forest, but he uses the same pronouns that the Monkey King used for just Dorothy!

"If I put an end to <u>your</u> enemy, will <u>you</u> bow down to me and obey me as King of the Forest?" inquired the Lion.

"Where is this great spider of <u>yours</u> now?" asked the Lion.

Wishes
by Sara Teasdale

I wish for such a lot of things
That never will come true -
And yet I want them all so much
I think they might, don't you?

I want a little kitty-cat
That's soft and tame and sweet,
And every day I watch and hope
I'll find one in the street.

But nursie says, "Come, walk along,
"Don't stand and stare like that" -
I'm only looking hard and hard
To try to find my cat.

And then I want a blue balloon
That tries to fly away,
I thought if I wished hard enough
That it would come some day.

One time when I was in the park
I knew that it would be
Beside the big old clock at home
A-waiting there for me -

And soon as we got home again,
I hurried thro' the hall,
And looked beside the big old clock -
It wasn't there at all.

I think I'll never wish again -
But then, what shall I do?
The wishes are a lot of fun
Altho' they don't come true.

The Ass and Its Shadow
An Aesop's Fable

    A Traveler had hired an Ass to carry him to a distant part of the country. The owner of the Ass went with the Traveler, walking beside him to drive the Ass and point out the way.

    The road led across a treeless plain where the Sun beat down fiercely. So intense did the heat become, that the Traveler at last decided to stop for a rest, and as there was no other shade to be found, the Traveler sat down in the shadow of the Ass.

    Now the heat had affected the Driver as much as it had the Traveler, and even more, for he had been walking. Wishing also to rest in the shade cast by the Ass, he began to quarrel with the Traveler, saying he had hired the Ass and not the shadow it cast.

    The two soon came to blows, and while they were fighting, the Ass took to its heels.

    In quarreling about the shadow we often lose the substance.

Exercise

In your workbook, underline the first person and second person pronouns from this passage:

> "Who are you?" asked the Scarecrow.

> Then a head showed itself over the rock and the same voice said, "This hill belongs to us, and we don't allow anyone to cross it."

Copywork

Literature

"This hill belongs to us, and we don't allow anyone to cross it."

Poetry—The Months

Dull November brings the blast,
Then the leaves are whirling fast.

Chill December brings the sleet,
Blazing fire, and Christmas treat.

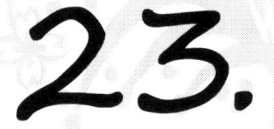

23. Definition: Homophones

- The Wonderful Wizard of Oz, Chapter 23

Homophones are words that have the same pronunciation but different meanings.

Do you know what it means for two words to have the same pronunciation? It means that both words sound exactly the same even though they mean different things. These words are homophones, and they are often spelled differently, too.

To, **too**, and **two** are all homophones. They all sound the same, but they have different meanings. Look at these sentences from *The Wonderful Wizard of Oz*:

> The house whirled around <u>two</u> or three times.
> Once Toto got <u>too</u> near the open trap door, and fell in.
> The other birds came <u>to</u> eat the corn <u>too</u>.

Blue and **blew** are also homophones. **Blue** is a color. **Blew** means something, like the wind, was blowing.

> There were big yellow and white and <u>blue</u> and purple blossoms.
> The soldier now <u>blew</u> upon a green whistle.

By, **buy**, and **bye** are all homophones. You're copying a poem **by** Sara Coleridge. At the store, your mother will **buy** groceries. And when you finish this lesson, you can wave **bye** to me!

Be aware of homophones when you are reading and writing and when a **bee** buzzes around your head. You can kiss your **dear** mother, but you probably shouldn't kiss a **deer**. While Dorothy and Toto are in Oz, you probably enjoy reading about **their** adventures, but would you want to go **there** yourself?

How Many Seconds
by Christina Rossetti

How many seconds in a minute?
Sixty, and no more in it.

How many minutes in an hour?
Sixty for sun and shower.

How many hours in a day?
Twenty-four for work and play.

How many days in a week?
Seven both to hear and speak.

How many weeks in a month?
Four, as the swift moon runn'th.

How many months in a year?
Twelve the almanac makes clear.

How many years in an age?
One hundred says the sage.

How many ages in time?
No one knows the rhyme.

The Astrologer
An Aesop's Fable

A man who lived a long time ago believed that he could read the future in the stars. He called himself an Astrologer, and spent his time at night gazing at the sky.

One evening he was walking along the open road outside the village. His eyes were fixed on the stars. He thought he saw there that the end of the world was at hand, when all at once, down he went into a hole full of mud and water.

There he stood up to his ears, in the muddy water, and madly clawing at the slippery sides of the hole in his effort to climb out.

His cries for help soon brought the villagers running. As they pulled him out of the mud, one of them said:

"You pretend to read the future in the stars, and yet you fail to see what is at your feet! This may teach you to pay more attention to what is right in front of you, and let the future take care of itself."

"What use is it," said another, "to read the stars, when you can't see what's right here on the earth?"

Take care of the little things and the big things will take care of themselves.

Exercise

In your workbook, underline the homophones from this passage:

"Why have you come to the South Country?"

"To see the Good Witch who rules here," she answered. "Will you take me to her?"

There were three homophones that we didn't talk about in this lesson. Can you find them? What are their homophones and how are they spelled? Write the homophone pairs on the homophone page in your workbook.

Copywork

Literature

"To see the Good Witch who rules here," she answered. "Will you take me to her?"

Maxim

Many hands make light work.

24. Narration: The Kid and the Wolf

- The Wonderful Wizard of Oz, Chapter 24

It's time for a narration. Your instructor will read this fable to you, and you will tell the story back to her while she writes it down for you. Then your instructor will write part of it for you to use as copywork.

The Kid and the Wolf
An Aesop's Fable

A frisky young Kid had been left by the herdsman on the thatched roof of a sheep shelter to keep him out of harm's way. The Kid was browsing near the edge of the roof, when he spied a Wolf and began to jeer at him, making faces and abusing him to his heart's content.

"I hear you," said the Wolf, "and I haven't the least grudge against you for what you say or do. When you are up there it is the roof that's talking, not you."

Do not say anything at any time that you would not say at all times.

Dawn
by Sara Teasdale

The greenish sky glows up in misty reds,
The purple shadows turn to brick and stone,
The dreams wear thin, men turn upon their beds,
And hear the milk-cart jangle by alone.

Copywork

Narration

Instructor: Write or print part of today's narration to use as copywork.

25. The Four Seasons

- The Blue Fairy Book: Snow-white and Rose-red

The four seasons are winter, spring, summer, and fall.

Your new poem to copy is called "The Four Seasons of the Year." The poem tells us when each season begins and about things we can expect in each season.

In March, spring begins. The weather begins to get warmer, birds return from the south to start families, and hibernating animals awake. Trees grow new leaves and plants begin to bloom.

In June, summer begins. Summer is the hottest time of year. Trees are full of leaves, collecting energy from the sun.

In September, fall begins. Fall is also called autumn. The weather begins to get cooler, leaves begin to change color, and crops are harvested. Hunting season begins in the fall, "when sportsmen mark at ev'ry bird."

In December, winter begins. Winter is the coldest time of year. Except for the evergreens, the trees are bare, and snow covers the ground in many parts of the country.

The names of the seasons are common nouns. Only capitalize the name of a season if it is the first word of a sentence, in a title, or the first word in the line of a poem.

Four Seasons of the Year*

On March the twenty-first is spring,
When little birds begin to sing;
Begin to build and hatch their brood,
And carefully provide them food.

Summer's the twenty-first of June,
The cuckoo changes then his tune;

All nature smiles, the fields look gay,
The weather's fair to make the hay.

September, on the twenty-third,
When sportsmen mark at ev'ry bird,
Autumn comes in; the fields are shorn,
The fruits are ripe; so is the corn.

Winter's cold frosts and northern blasts,
The season is we mention last;
The date of which in truth we must
Fix for December: twenty-first.

*This poem appeared in The Infant System (1852) by Samuel Wilderspin

The Bees and Wasps, and the Hornet
An Aesop's Fable

A store of honey had been found in a hollow tree, and the Wasps declared positively that it belonged to them. The Bees were just as sure that the treasure was theirs. The argument grew very pointed, and it looked as if the affair could not be settled without a battle, when at last, with much good sense, they agreed to let a judge decide the matter. So they brought the case before the Hornet, justice of the peace in that part of the woods.

When the Judge called the case, witnesses declared that they had seen certain winged creatures in the neighborhood of the hollow tree, who hummed loudly, and whose bodies were striped, yellow and black, like Bees.

Counsel for the Wasps immediately insisted that this description fitted his clients exactly.

Such evidence did not help Judge Hornet to any decision, so he adjourned court for six weeks to give him time to think it over. When the case came up again, both sides had a large number of witnesses. An Ant was first to take the stand, and was about to be cross-examined, when a wise old Bee addressed the Court.

"Your honor," he said, "the case has now been pending for six weeks. If it is not decided soon, the honey will not be fit for anything. I move that the Bees and the Wasps be both instructed to build a honey comb. Then we shall soon see to whom the honey really belongs."

The Wasps protested loudly. Wise Judge Hornet quickly understood why they did so: They knew they could not build a honey comb and fill it with honey.

"It is clear," said the Judge, "who made the comb and who could not have made it. The honey belongs to the Bees."

Ability proves itself by deeds.

Exercise

In your workbook, underline the first person and second person pronouns from this passage:

"Where are you going to, dear bear?" asked Snow-white.

"I must go to the wood and protect my treasure from the wicked dwarfs. In winter, when the earth is frozen hard, they are obliged to remain underground."

Remember that an antecedent is the noun that has been replaced by a pronoun. What nouns are replaced by the pronouns in these sentences?

Copywork

Literature

"In winter, when the earth is frozen hard, they are obliged to remain underground."

Poetry—The Four Seasons

On March the twenty-first is spring,
When little birds begin to sing;
Begin to build and hatch their brood,
And carefully provide them food.

26. Second Person Pronouns

- The Blue Fairy Book: East of the Sun and West of the Moon

**A pronoun is a word used
in the place of a noun.**

A pronoun replaces a noun in a sentence. When you are speaking to someone, you use second person pronouns to replace that person's name.

The second person pronouns are **you**, **your**, **yours**. Whether we are speaking to one person or to many people, we use the pronouns **you**, **your**, and **yours** to refer to the person or people to whom we are speaking.

Complete each of the following sentences from "East of the Sun and West of the Moon" using second person pronouns.

"Will _____ give me _____ youngest daughter?" said the White Bear.

"How much do _____ want for that gold apple of _____, girl?" said she.

When the Frost is on the Punkin
by James Whitcomb Riley

When the frost is on the punkin and the fodder's in the shock,
And you hear the kyouck and gobble of the struttin' turkey-cock,
And the clackin' of the guineys, and the cluckin' of the hens,
And the rooster's hallylooyer as he tiptoes on the fence;
O, it's then's the times a feller is a-feelin' at his best,
With the risin' sun to greet him from a night of peaceful rest,
As he leaves the house, bareheaded, and goes to feed the stock,
When the frost is on the punkin and the fodder's in the shock.

They's something kindo' harty-like about the atmusfere
When the heat of summer's over and the coolin' fall is here —
Of course we miss the flowers, and the blossums on the trees,
And the mumble of the hummin'-birds and buzzin' of the bees;
But the air's so appetizin'; and the landscape through the haze

Of a crisp and sunny morning of the airly autumn days
Is a pictur' that no painter has the colorin' to mock —
When the frost is on the punkin and the fodder's in the shock.

The husky, rusty russel of the tossels of the corn,
And the raspin' of the tangled leaves, as golden as the morn;
The stubble in the furries — kindo' lonesome-like, but still
A-preachin' sermons to us of the barns they growed to fill;
The strawsack in the medder, and the reaper in the shed;
The hosses in theyr stalls below — the clover overhead! —
O, it sets my hart a-clickin' like the tickin' of a clock,
When the frost is on the punkin, and the fodder's in the shock!

Then your apples all is gethered, and the ones a feller keeps
Is poured around the celler-floor in red and yeller heaps;
And your cider-makin's over, and your wimmern-folks is through
With their mince and apple-butter, and theyr souse and saussage, too!
I don't know how to tell it — but ef sich a thing could be
As the Angles wantin' boardin', and they'd call around on me —
I'd want to 'commodate 'em — all the whole-indurin' flock —
When the frost is on the punkin and the fodder's in the shock!

The Man and the Satyr
An Aesop's Fable

 A long time ago a Man met a Satyr in the forest and succeeded in making friends with him. The two soon became the best of comrades, living together in the Man's hut. But one cold winter evening, as they were walking homeward, the Satyr saw the Man blow on his fingers.
 "Why do you do that?" asked the Satyr.
 "To warm my hands," the Man replied.
 When they reached home the Man prepared two bowls of porridge. These he placed steaming hot on the table, and the comrades sat down very cheerfully to enjoy the meal. But much to the Satyr's surprise, the Man began to blow into his bowl of porridge.
 "Why do you do that?" he asked.
 "To cool my porridge," replied the Man.
 The Satyr sprang hurriedly to his feet and made for the door.
 "Goodby," he said, "I've seen enough. A fellow that blows hot and cold in the same breath cannot be friends with me!"
 The man who talks for both sides is not to be trusted by either.

Exercise

In your workbook, write N above each of the nouns, V above each of the verbs, and underline the first person and second person pronouns from this passage. If a proper noun has more than one word, make arms stretched out to include the whole thing, like this: ——N——

> "Very well then," said the North Wind. "But you must sleep here tonight, for if we are ever to get there we must have the day before us."

Do you remember what an antecedent is? An antecedent is the noun that has been replaced by a pronoun. What nouns are replaced by the pronouns in these sentences?

Copywork

Literature

"But you must sleep here tonight, for if we are ever to get there we must have the day before us."

Bible—Colossians 3:2

Set your minds on things that are above, not on things that are on earth.

Woman Baking Bread by Jean-Francois Millet

Picture Study

1. Read the title and the name of the artist. Study the picture for several minutes, then put the picture away.

2. Describe the picture.

3. Look at the picture again. Do you notice any details that you missed before? What do you like or dislike about this painting? Does it remind you of anything?

27. Abbreviations: States; Picture Study: Woman Baking Bread

- The Blue Fairy Book: Beauty and the Beast

Remember that an abbreviation is a short way to write a word. There are fifty states in the United States of America, and the Post Office has assigned each state its own special two letter abbreviation. This makes
it easier for the Post Office to deliver mail. The abbreviations for states are a little different from other abbreviations. When we write an abbreviation for a state, we capitalize both letters, and we don't use a period at the end.

Look at the state abbreviations on the next page. In which state were you born? In which state do you now live? What are the abbreviations for those states?

The Double
by Walter de la Mare

I curtseyed to the dovecote.
   I curtseyed to the well.
I twirled me round and round about,
   The morning sweets to smell.
When out I came from spinning so,
   Lo, betwixt green and blue
Was the ghost of me—a Fairy Child—
   A-dancing—dancing, too.

Nought was of her wearing
   That is the earth's array.
Her thistledown feet beat airy fleet
   Yet set no blade astray.
The gossamer shining dews of
   June Showed grey against the green;
Yet never so much as a bird-claw print
   Of footfall to be seen.

Fading in the mounting sun
   That image soon did pine.
Fainter than moonlight thinned the locks

> That shone as clear as mine.
> Vanished! Vanished! O, sad it is
>   To spin and spin—in vain;
> And never to see the ghost of me
>   A-dancing there again.

Exercise

In your workbook, write N above each of the nouns and V above each of the verbs from this passage:

> Then he went down into the garden, and though it was winter everywhere else, here the sun shone, and the birds sang, and the flowers bloomed, and the air was soft and sweet.

Copywork

Literature

> Here the sun shone, and the birds sang, and the flowers bloomed, and the air was soft and sweet.

Alabama	AL	Montana	MT
Alaska	AK	Nebraska	NE
Arizona	AZ	Nevada	NV
Arkansas	AR	New Hampshire	NH
California	CA	New Jersey	NJ
Colorado	CO	New Mexico	NM
Connecticut	CT	New York	NY
Delaware	DE	North Carolina	NC
Florida	FL	North Dakota	ND
Georgia	GA	Ohio	OH
Hawaii	HI	Oklahoma	OK
Idaho	ID	Oregon	OR
Illinois	IL	Pennsylvania	PA
Indiana	IN	Rhode Island	RI
Iowa	IA	South Carolina	SC
Kansas	KS	South Dakota	SD
Kentucky	KY	Tennessee	TN
Louisiana	LA	Texas	TX
Maine	ME	Utah	UT
Maryland	MD	Vermont	VT
Massachusetts	MA	Virginia	VA
Michigan	MI	Washington	WA
Minnesota	MN	West Virginia	WV
Mississippi	MS	Wisconsin	WI
Missouri	MO	Wyoming	WY
		District Of Columbia	DC

28. Addresses

- The Blue Fairy Book: Little Red Riding-Hood

You live on a street, in a town or city, in a state, in a country.

Your address tells people where you live. When you write an address, you must include all of this information for people to be able to find the correct house.

First we write the street address. Do you know the name of the street on which you live? Many other people live on your street, too. That's why each house has a number. To write the street address, we first write the house number, then we write the street name. A street name is a proper noun, so it must begin with a capital letter.

    1600 Pennsylvania Ave. NW

The Post Office has divided the country into small areas, and they've given each area a special number called a zip code. The zip code tells in which part of the United States a person lives, and it makes it easier for the Post Office to deliver mail. So on the next line, we write the name of the town or city and the abbreviation for the state. We separate the city and the state with a comma. Then we write the zip code.

    Washington, DC 20500

Put it all together, and we have a complete address:

    1600 Pennsylvania Ave. NW
    Washington, DC 20500

This is the address of the White House, home of the President.

Instructor: Add your address to a memory card for the child to memorize.

Pippa's Song
by Robert Browning

The year's at the spring,
And day's at the morn;
Morning's at seven;
The hill-side's dew-pearl'd;
The lark's on the wing;
The snail's on the thorn;
God's in His heaven—
All's right with the world!

The Fox and the Crow
An Aesop's Fable

One bright morning as the Fox was following his sharp nose through the wood in search of a bite to eat, he saw a Crow on the limb of a tree overhead. This was by no means the first Crow the Fox had ever seen. What caught his attention this time and made him stop for a second look, was that the lucky Crow held a bit of cheese in her beak.

"No need to search any farther," thought sly Master Fox. "Here is a dainty bite for my breakfast."

Up he trotted to the foot of the tree in which the Crow was sitting, and looking up admiringly, he cried, "Good-morning, beautiful creature!"

The Crow, her head cocked on one side, watched the Fox suspiciously. But she kept her beak tightly closed on the cheese and did not return his greeting.

"What a charming creature she is!" said the Fox. "How her feathers shine! What a beautiful form and what splendid wings! Such a wonderful Bird should have a very lovely voice, since everything else about her is so perfect. Could she sing just one song, I know I should hail her Queen of Birds."

Listening to these flattering words, the Crow forgot all her suspicion, and also her breakfast. She wanted very much to be called Queen of Birds.

So she opened her beak wide to utter her loudest caw, and down fell the cheese straight into the Fox's open mouth.

"Thank you," said Master Fox sweetly, as he walked off. "Though it is cracked, you have a voice sure enough. But where are your wits?"

The flatterer lives at the expense of those who will listen to him.

Exercise

In your workbook, write N above each of the nouns and V above each of the verbs from this passage:

> The poor child, who did not know it was dangerous to stay and hear a wolf talk, said to him, "I am going to see my grandmamma and carry her a custard and a little pot of butter from my mamma."

Copywork

Address

Instructor: Write or print the home address to copy.

Poetry—The Four Seasons

Summer's the twenty-first of June,
The cuckoo changes then his tune;
All nature smiles, the fields look gay,
The weather's fair to make the hay.

29. Third Person Singular Pronouns

- The Blue Fairy Book: Rumpelstiltzkin

A pronoun is a word used in the place of a noun.

The first person pronouns are: **I, me, my, mine, we, us, our, ours**. We use first person pronouns when we speak of ourselves. The antecedent—the noun being replaced—of a first person pronoun is the name of the person speaking.

The second person pronouns are: **you, your, yours**. Second person pronouns take the place of the name of the person to whom we are speaking.

Today, we will learn about third person pronouns. We use third person pronouns when we speak of everyone and everything else. The third person singular pronouns are **he, him, his, she, her, hers, it, its**. Remember that singular means only one.

Look at these sentences from "Rumpelstiltzkin." The third person singular pronouns are underlined.

"<u>She</u> is only a miller's daughter, <u>it</u> is true," <u>he</u> thought.

<u>He</u> straightway made <u>her</u> <u>his</u> wife.

Then <u>he</u> closed the door behind <u>him</u> and left <u>her</u> alone inside.

Complete these sentences with a third person singular pronoun.

The King was greedy. _____ was greedy.

The miller's daughter had a ring. The ring was _____.

The straw was spun into gold. _____ was spun into gold.

The Queen guessed Rumpelstiltzkin's name. _____ guessed _____ name.

Summer Evening
by Walter de la Mare

The sandy cat by the Farmer's chair
Mews at his knee for dainty fare;
Old Rover in his moss-greened house
Mumbles a bone, and barks at a mouse
In the dewy fields the cattle lie
Chewing the cud 'neath a fading sky
Dobbin at manger pulls his hay:
Gone is another summer's day.

The Lion, the Ass, and the Fox
An Aesop's Fable

A Lion, an Ass, and a Fox were hunting in company, and caught a large quantity of game. The Ass was asked to divide the spoil. This he did very fairly, giving each an equal share.

The Fox was well satisfied, but the Lion flew into a great rage over it, and with one stroke of his huge paw, he added the Ass to the pile of slain.

Then he turned to the Fox.

"You divide it," he roared angrily.

The Fox wasted no time in talking. He quickly piled all the game into one great heap. From this he took a very small portion for himself, such undesirable bits as the horns and hoofs of a mountain goat, and the end of an ox tail.

The Lion now recovered his good humor entirely.

"Who taught you to divide so fairly?" he asked pleasantly.

"I learned a lesson from the Ass," replied the Fox, carefully edging away.

Learn from the misfortunes of others.

Exercise

In your workbook, underline the first person, second person, and third person singular pronouns from this passage:

> Then the Queen began to cry and sob so bitterly that the little man was sorry for her, and said: "I will give you three days to guess my name, and if you find it out in that time you may keep your child."

What is the antecedent (the noun being replaced) of each pronoun?

Copywork

Literature

> "I will give you three days to guess my name, and if you find it out in that time you may keep your child."

Maxim

> Actions speak louder than words.

30. Narration: The Boy Bathing

- The Blue Fairy Book: Toads and Diamonds

It's time for a narration. Your instructor will read this fable to you, and you will tell the story back to her while she writes it down for you. Then your instructor will write part of it for you to use as copywork.

The Boy Bathing
An Aesop's Fable retold by J. H. Stickney

A little Boy once went in bathing where the water was too deep for him. When found himself sinking, he cried out to a Man who was passing by to come and help him.

"Can't you swim?" asked the Man.

"No," replied the Boy, "I don't know how."

"How foolish you were, then," said the Man, "to go into deep water! Didn't you know better?"

"Oh, good sir, please help me now, or I shall drown!" cried the Boy. "You can scold me when I am safe on shore again."

The First Bluebird
by James Whitcomb Riley

Jest rain and snow! and rain again!
And dribble! drip! and blow!
Then snow! and thaw! and slush! and then
Some more rain and snow!

This morning I was 'most afeard
To wake up when, I jing!
I seen the sun shine out and heerd
The first bluebird of Spring!

Mother she'd raised the winder some;
And in acrost the orchurd come,
Soft as a angel's wing,
A breezy, treesy, beesy hum,
Too sweet fer anything!

The winter's shroud was rent a-part
The sun bust forth in glee,
And when that bluebird sung, my hart
Hopped out o' bed with me!

Copywork

Narration

Instructor: Write or print part of today's narration to use as copywork.

31. Third Person Plural Pronouns

- The Blue Fairy Book: Hansel and Grettel

A pronoun is a word used in the place of a noun.

Remember that plural means more than one. The third person plural pronouns are: **they, them, their, theirs**. We use third person plural pronouns when we speak of more than one person or object.

We use the first person pronouns when we speak of ourselves: **I, me, my, mine, we, us, our, ours.**

We use the second person pronouns to replace the name of the person to whom we are speaking: **you, your, yours.**

We use the third person pronouns to speak of others: he, him, his, she, her, hers, it, its, they, them, their, theirs.

Use third person pronouns to complete these sentences.

The woodcutter left his children in the forest. _____ left _____ in the forest.

Hansel and Grettel had some bread. The bread was _____.

The best food was for Hansel. The best food was for _____.

Grettel pushed the witch into the oven. _____ pushed _____ into the oven.

The children and the woodcutter lived happily ever after. _____ lived happily ever after.

Answer To A Child's Question
by Samuel Taylor Coleridge

Do you ask what the birds say? The sparrow, the dove,
The linnet, and thrush say, "I love, and I love!"
In the winter they're silent, the wind is so strong;
What it says I don't know, but it sings a loud song.

But green leaves, and blossoms, and sunny warm weather,
And singing and loving—all come back together.
But the lark is so brimful of gladness and love,
The green fields below him, the blue sky above,
That he sings, and he sings, and forever sings he,
"I love my love, and my love loves me."

The Ass and the Load of Salt
An Aesop's Fable

A Merchant, driving his Ass homeward from the seashore with a heavy load of salt, came to a river crossed by a shallow ford. They had crossed this river many times before without accident, but this time the Ass slipped and fell when halfway over. And when the Merchant at last got him to his feet, much of the salt had melted away. Delighted to find how much lighter his burden had become, the Ass finished the journey very gayly.

Next day the Merchant went for another load of salt. On the way home the Ass, remembering what had happened at the ford, purposely let himself fall into the water, and again got rid of most of his burden.

The angry Merchant immediately turned about and drove the Ass back to the seashore, where he loaded him with two great baskets of sponges. At the ford the Ass again tumbled over; but when he had scrambled to his feet, it was a very disconsolate Ass that dragged himself homeward under a load ten times heavier than before.

The same measures will not suit all circumstances.

Exercise

In your workbook, underline the pronouns from this passage:

> Hansel bent down and filled his pocket with as many of them as he could cram in. Then he went back and said to Grettel, "Be comforted, my dear little sister, and go to sleep. God will not desert us."

What is the antecedent (the noun being replaced) of each pronoun?

Copywork

Literature

> "Be comforted, my dear little sister, and go to sleep. God will not desert us."

Poetry—The Four Seasons

> September, on the twenty-third,
> When sportsmen mark at ev'ry bird,
> Autumn comes in; the fields are shorn,
> The fruits are ripe; so is the corn.

32. Phone Numbers

- The Blue Fairy Book: The Story of Pretty Goldilocks

No one else has your exact phone number. Every phone number is unique.

Your phone number has ten digits. The first three digits are called the area code. Like a zip code, an area code is the same for everyone who lives in a certain area of the country. You don't have to dial the area code when you call someone who has the same area code as you. You do have to dial the area code for people who live in different area codes. The other seven digits are your phone number. When we write the area code with the phone number, we separate the area code with punctuation marks called parentheses. We put a dash between the first three digits of the phone number and the last four digits, like this:

(817) 776—9240

Today you will start memorizing your phone number. Practice saying it three times everyday until you can say it without looking.

Note to instructor: Add the home phone number to a memory card for the child to memorize. Once the home phone number is memorized, add additional memory cards for parents' work phone numbers, mobile numbers, 911, and/or any other phone numbers the child might need in an emergency. You might consider allowing the child to dial the number on occasion when you call friends or relatives and to start his own book of addresses and phone numbers. You might also want to take this opportunity to point out that phone numbers should be kept private unless the child has permission to give them out.

Spring Night
by Sara Teasdale

The park is filled with night and fog,
The veils are drawn about the world,
The drowsy lights along the paths
Are dim and pearled.

Gold and gleaming the empty streets,

Gold and gleaming the misty lake,
The mirrored lights like sunken swords,
Glimmer and shake.

Oh, is it not enough to be
Here with this beauty over me?
My throat should ache with praise, and I
Should kneel in joy beneath the sky.
Oh, beauty are you not enough?

The Two Pots
An Aesop's Fable

Two Pots, one of brass and the other of clay, stood together on the hearthstone. One day the Brass Pot proposed to the Earthen Pot that they go out into the world together. But the Earthen Pot excused himself, saying that it would be wiser for him to stay in the corner by the fire.

"It would take so little to break me," he said. "You know how fragile I am. The least shock is sure to shatter me!"

"Don't let that keep you at home," urged the Brass Pot. "I shall take very good care of you. If we should happen to meet anything hard I will step between and save you."

So the Earthen Pot at last consented, and the two set out side by side, jolting along on three stubby legs first to this side, then to that, and bumping into each other at every step.

The Earthen Pot could not survive that sort of companionship very long. They had not gone ten paces before the Earthen Pot cracked, and at the next jolt he flew into a thousand pieces.

Equals make the best friends.

Exercise

In your workbook, write N above each of the nouns and V above each of the verbs from this passage. If a proper noun has more than one word, make arms stretched out to include the whole thing, like this: ———N———

"You saved my life in the meadow by the willow tree, and I promised that I would repay you. Take this, it is Princess Goldilocks's ring."

Copywork

Phone Number

Instructor: Write the home phone number in the workbook for the child to copy several times.

Bible—Psalm 119:11

Your word I have treasured in my heart,

That I may not sin against You.

Woman Hanging Her Laundry by Jean-Francois Millet

Picture Study

1. Read the title and the name of the artist. Study the picture for several minutes, then put the picture away.

2. Describe the picture.

3. Look at the picture again. Do you notice any details that you missed before? What do you like or dislike about this painting? Does it remind you of anything?

33. State of Being Verbs; Picture Study: Woman Hanging Her Laundry

- The Blue Fairy Book: Prince Darling

A verb is a word that shows action or state of being.

We've already learned about verbs that express action. Today, we'll learn about verbs that show state of being.

The state of being verbs are: am, are, is, was, were, be, being, been.

State of being verbs do not show action, nor do they tell anything about someone or something. A state of being verb only says that someone or something exists.

> I am.
> You are.
> He is.
> She was.
> They were.

State of being verbs can be used to answer questions, but they do not give any additional information. Use state of being verbs to complete these sentences.

Are you ready to complete this lesson? I _____.

Am I looking lovely today? You _____.

Is the kitten cute and furry? It _____.

Was the book fun to read? It _____.

Were the children playing? They _____.

Daffadowndilly
by Christina Rossetti

Growing in the vale
By the uplands hilly,
Growing straight and frail,
Lady Daffadowndilly.

In a golden crown,
And a scant green gown
While the spring blows chilly,
Lady Daffadown,
Sweet Daffadowndilly.

Exercise

In your workbook, underline the pronouns from this passage:

> "What good would it do him to be rich, or handsome, or to possess all the kingdoms of the world if he were wicked? You know he would still be unhappy. Only a good man can be really contented."

What is the antecedent (the noun being replaced) of each pronoun?

Copywork

Literature

> "You know he would still be unhappy. Only a good man can be really contented."

34. Contractions

- The Blue Fairy Book: The History of Jack the Giant-Killer

To contract means to make smaller. Sometimes, we take two words and make one smaller word. We call this a contraction.

When we make a contraction, we leave some letters out of the new word. We use an apostrophe to show where the missing letters would go.

I am	I'm	I will	I'll
we are	we're	we will	we'll
you are	you're	you will	you'll
he is	he's	he will	he'll
she is	she's	she will	she'll
it is	it's	it will	it'll
they are	they're	they will	they'll

It'll is a contraction, but it's not used very often.

Read each pair of words and its contraction. Which letters are missing from each contraction?

Autumn Fires
by Robert Louis Stevenson

In the other gardens
And all up the vale,
From the autumn bonfires
See the smoke trail!

Pleasant summer over
And all the summer flowers,

The red fire blazes,
The grey smoke towers.

Sing a song of seasons!
Something bright in all!
Flowers in the summer,
Fires in the fall!

The Eagle and the Kite
An Aesop's Fable

An Eagle sat high in the branches of a great Oak. She seemed very sad and drooping for an Eagle. A Kite saw her.

"Why do you look so woebegone?" asked the Kite.

"I want to get married," replied the Eagle, "and I can't find a mate who can provide for me as I should like."

"Take me," said the Kite. "I am very strong, stronger even than you!"

"Do you really think you can provide for me?" asked the Eagle eagerly.

"Why, of course," replied the Kite. "That would be a very simple matter. I am so strong I can carry away an Ostrich in my talons as if it were a feather!"

The Eagle accepted the Kite immediately. But after the wedding, when the Kite flew away to find something to eat for his bride, all he had when he returned was a tiny Mouse.

"Is that the Ostrich you talked about?" said the Eagle in disgust.

"To win you I would have said and promised anything," replied the Kite.

Everything is fair in love.

Exercise

In your workbook, circle the contraction and underline the pronouns from this passage:

> He then blew such a tantivy that the giant awoke and came out of his den, crying out, "You saucy villain! You shall pay for this. I'll broil you for my breakfast!"

Copywork

Contractions

In your workbook, write the contraction for each pair of words.

I am	we are	you are
he is	she is	it is
they are	I will	we will
he will	she will	they will

Poetry—The Four Seasons

> Winter's cold frosts and northern blasts,
> The season is we mention last;
> The date of which in truth we must
> Fix for December: twenty-first.

35. Review: Capitalization

- The Blue Fairy Book: The Forty Thieves

Can you remember when to capitalize words? Let's review.

- Capitalize proper nouns.

    Thomas Jefferson, New York City, Rocky Mountains—these are all proper nouns, so we capitalize them.

- Capitalize the pronoun I.

    The pronoun I is always capitalized. Never write the pronoun I as a lower-case letter.

- Capitalize the first word in a sentence.

- Capitalize the first word of every line of a poem.

- Capitalize titles.

    The Blue Fairy Book— this is the title of a book, so we capitalize every word except for little ones like a, an, the, and, of, or. Only capitalize a little word in a title when it is the first word in the title. These rules are the same for the title of a poem.

Bed in Summer
by Robert Louis Stevenson

In winter I get up at night
And dress by yellow candle-light.
In summer quite the other way,
I have to go to bed by day.

I have to go to bed and see
The birds still hopping on the tree,
Or hear the grown-up people's feet
Still going past me in the street.

And does it not seem hard to you,
When all the sky is clear and blue,
And I should like so much to play,
To have to go to bed by day?

The Miller, His Son, and the Ass
An Aesop's Fable

One day, a long time ago, an old Miller and his Son were on their way to market with an Ass which they hoped to sell. They drove him very slowly, for they thought they would have a better chance to sell him if they kept him in good condition. As they walked along the highway some travelers laughed loudly at them.

"What foolishness," cried one, "to walk when they might as well ride. The most stupid of the three is not the one you would expect it to be."

The Miller did not like to be laughed at, so he told his son to climb up and ride.

They had gone a little farther along the road, when three merchants passed by.

"Oho, what have we here?" they cried. "Respect old age, young man! Get down, and let the old man ride."

Though the Miller was not tired, he made the boy get down and climbed up himself to ride, just to please the Merchants.

At the next turnstile they overtook some women carrying market baskets loaded with vegetables and other things to sell.

"Look at the old fool," exclaimed one of them. "Perched on the Ass, while that poor boy has to walk."

The Miller felt a bit vexed, but to be agreeable he told the Boy to climb up behind him.

They had no sooner started out again than a loud shout went up from another company of people on the road.

"What a crime," cried one, "to load up a poor dumb beast like that! They look more able to carry the poor creature, than he to carry them."

"They must be on their way to sell the poor thing's hide," said another.

The Miller and his Son quickly scrambled down, and a short time later, the market place was thrown into an uproar as the two came along carrying the Donkey slung from a pole. A great crowd of people ran out to get a closer look at the strange sight.

The Ass did not dislike being carried, but so many people came up to point at him and laugh and shout, that he began to kick and bray, and then, just as they were crossing a bridge, the ropes that held him gave way, and down he tumbled into the river.

The poor Miller now set out sadly for home. By trying to please everybody, he had pleased nobody, and lost his Ass besides.

If you try to please all, you please none.

Exercise

In your workbook, write N above each of the nouns and V above each of the verbs from this passage. If a proper noun has more than one word, make arms stretched out to include the whole thing, like this: ———N———

Then Ali Baba climbed down and went to the door concealed among the bushes, and said, "Open, Sesame!"

Copywork

Literature

Then Ali Baba climbed down and went to the door concealed among the bushes, and said, "Open, Sesame!"

Maxim

A penny saved is a penny earned.

36. Narration: The Boys and the Frogs

- The Blue Fairy Book: Aladdin and the Wonderful Lamp

It's time for a narration. Your instructor will read this fable to you, and you will tell the story back to her while she writes it down for you. Then your instructor will write part of it for you to use as copywork.

The Boys and the Frogs
An Aesop's Fable

Some boys were playing one day at the edge of a pond in which lived a family of Frogs. The Boys amused themselves by throwing stones into the pond so as to make them skip on top of the water.

The stones were flying thick and fast and the Boys were enjoying themselves very much; but the poor Frogs in the pond were trembling with fear.

At last one of the Frogs, the oldest and bravest, put his head out of the water, and said, "Oh, please, dear children, stop your cruel play! Though it may be fun for you, it means death to us!"

Always stop to think whether your fun may not be the cause of another's unhappiness.

The Old Swimmin'-Hole
by James Whitcomb Riley

Oh! the old swimmin'-hole! whare the crick so still and deep
Looked like a baby-river that was laying half asleep,
And the gurgle of the worter round the drift jest below
Sounded like the laugh of something we onc't ust to know
Before we could remember anything but the eyes
Of the angels lookin' out as we left Paradise;
But the merry days of youth is beyond our controle,
And it's hard to part ferever with the old swimmin'-hole.

Oh! the old swimmin'-hole! In the happy days of yore,
When I ust to lean above it on the old sickamore,
Oh! it showed me a face in its warm sunny tide
That gazed back at me so gay and glorified,

It made me love myself, as I leaped to cares
My shadder smilin' up at me with sich tenderness.
But them days is past and gone, and old Time's tuck his toll
From the old man come back to the old swimmin'-hole.

Oh! the old swimmin'-hole! In the long, lazy days
When the humdrum of school made so many run-a-ways,
How pleasant was the jurney down the old dusty lane,
Whare the tracks of our bare feet was all printed so plane
You could tell by the dent of the heel and the sole
They was lots o' fun on hands at the old swimmin'-hole.
But the lost joys is past! Let your tears in sorrow roll
Like the rain that ust to dapple up the old swimmin'-hole.

Thare the bullrushes growed, and the cattails so tall,
And the sunshine and shadder fell over it all;
And it mottled the worter with amber and gold
Tel the glad lilies rocked in the ripples that rolled;
And the snake-feeder's four gauzy wings fluttered by
Like the ghost of a daisy dropped out of the sky,
Or a wownded apple-blossom in the breeze's controle
As it cut acrost some orchurd to'rds the old swimmin'-hole.

Oh! the old swimmin'-hole! When I last saw the place,
The scenes was all changed, like the change in my face;
The bridge of the railroad now crosses the spot
Whare the old divin'-log lays sunk and ferfot.
And I stray down the banks whare the trees ust to be —
But never again will theyr shade shelter me!
And I wish in my sorrow I could strip to the soul,
And dive off in my grave like the old swimmin'-hole.

Copywork

Narration

Instructor: Write or print part of today's narration to use as copywork.

37. The Days of the Week

- The Blue Fairy Book: Prince Hyacinth and the Dear Little Princess

**The days of the week are
Sunday, Monday, Tuesday, Wednesday,
Thursday, Friday, and Saturday.**

Start memorizing the days of the week. There are seven days in a week, and you have a silly Mother Goose rhyme to copy to learn to write them all.

Have you ever wondered where we got the names for the days of the week? Many of them come from the names of gods in Norse and Germanic mythology. These are listed below.

Remember that an abbreviation is a shorter way to write a word. Just as there are abbreviations for the months of the year, there are also abbreviations for the days of the week. Because the days of the week are proper nouns, each abbreviation must begin with a capital letter. Don't forget the period on the end!

Sunday	Sun.	Sun's day
Monday	Mon.	Moon's day
Tuesday	Tue. or Tues.	Tiw's (Tyr's) day
Wednesday	Wed.	Woden's (Odin's) day
Thursday	Thu. or Thurs.	Thor's day
Friday	Fri.	Frigg's day
Saturday	Sat.	Saturn's day

Solomon Grundy
A Mother Goose Rhyme

Solomon Grundy,
Born on a Monday,
Christened on Tuesday,

Married on Wednesday,
Took ill on Thursday,
Worse on Friday,
Died on Saturday,
Buried on Sunday.
This is the end
Of Solomon Grundy.

The Stag, the Sheep, and the Wolf
An Aesop's Fable

One day a Stag came to a Sheep and asked her to lend him a measure of wheat. The Sheep knew him for a very swift runner, who could easily take himself out of reach, were he so inclined. So she asked him if he knew someone who would answer for him.

"Yes, yes," answered the Stag confidently, "the Wolf has promised to be my surety."

"The Wolf!" exclaimed the Sheep indignantly. "Do you think I would trust you on such security? I know the Wolf! He takes what he wants and runs off with it without paying. As for you, you can use your legs so well that I should have little chance of collecting the debt if I had to catch you for it!"

Two blacks do not make a white.

Exercise

In your workbook, write N above each of the nouns and V above each of the verbs from this passage:

"You see how self-love keeps us from knowing our own defects of mind and body."

Copywork

Literature

"You see how self-love keeps us from knowing our own defects of mind and body."

Abbreviations—Days

Sun.   Mon.   Tue.   Wed.

Thu.   Fri.   Sat.

Poetry—Solomon Grundy

Solomon Grundy,
Born on a Monday,

38. State of Being Verbs; Review: Pronouns

- Peter Pan, Chapter 1

The state of being verbs are:
am, are, is, was, were, be, being, been.

State of being verbs do not show action, they only show that someone or something exists. Use state of being verbs to answer these questions:

Are you enjoying the book Peter Pan? I _____.

Am I reading this lesson? You _____.

Is Nana a dog? She _____.

Was Peter coming in the window? He _____.

Were the children sleeping? They _____.

Personal Pronouns

First person pronouns replace the name of the person speaking. The first person pronouns are: I, me, my, mine, we, us, our, ours.

Second person pronouns replace the name of the person to whom one is speaking. The second person pronouns are: you, your, yours.

Third person pronouns replace the name of everyone and everything else. The third person pronouns are: he, him, his, she, her, hers, it, its, they, them, their, theirs.

Peter broke through. _____ broke through.

Nana is a dog. _____ is a dog.

Peter was in the children's room. _____ was in _____ room.

Mrs. Darling sat by the fire. _____ sat by the fire.

"Wendy forgot," said Wendy. "_____ forgot," said Wendy.

Monday's Child
A Mother Goose Rhyme

Monday's child is fair of face,
Tuesday's child is full of grace,
Wednesday's child is full of woe,
Thursday's child has far to go,
Friday's child is loving and giving,
Saturday's child works hard for a living,
And the child that's born on the Sabbath day
Is blithe and bonny and good and gay.

Exercise

In your workbook, underline the pronouns from this passage:

> Mrs. Darling first heard of Peter when she was tidying up her children's minds. It is the nightly custom of every good mother after her children are asleep to rummage in their minds and put things straight for next morning.

What is the antecedent (the noun being replaced) of each pronoun?

Copywork

Literature

> Mrs. Darling first heard of Peter when she was tidying up her children's minds.

Bible—Ephesians 4:32

> Be kind to one another, tender-hearted, forgiving each other, just as God in Christ also has forgiven you.

Fresh Eggs by Winslow Homer

Picture Study

1. Read the title and the name of the artist. Study the picture for several minutes, then put the picture away.

2. Describe the picture.

3. Look at the picture again. Do you notice any details that you missed before? What do you like or dislike about this painting? Does it remind you of anything?

39. Contractions; Picture Study: Fresh Eggs

- Peter Pan, Chapter 2

Remember that when we make a contraction, we leave some letters out of the new word. We use an apostrophe to show where the missing letters would go.

is not	isn't	are not	aren't
was not	wasn't	were not	weren't
do not	don't	does not	doesn't
did not	didn't	have not	haven't
has not	hasn't	had not	hadn't
cannot	can't	could not	couldn't
will not	won't	would not	wouldn't
shall not	shan't	should not	shouldn't

All of the above contraction use the word **not**. Which letter is missing from the contractions?

Look closely at the contractions for **will not** and **shall not**. Did you notice that they are slightly different from the rest?

Five Eyes
by Walter de la Mare

In Hans' old Mill his three black cats
Watch the bins for the thieving rats.
Whisker and claw, they crouch in the night,
Their five eyes smouldering green and bright:

Squeaks from the flour sacks, squeaks from where
The cold wind stirs on the empty stair,
Squeaking and scampering, everywhere.
Then down they pounce, now in, now out,
At whisking tail, and sniffing snout;
While lean old Hans he snores away
Till peep of light at break of day;
Then up he climbs to his creaking mill,
Out come his cats all grey with meal —
Jekkel, and Jessup, and one-eyed Jill.

Exercise

In your workbook, underline the contractions from this passage:

> "Nana, it isn't six o'clock yet. Oh dear, oh dear, I shan't love you any more, Nana. I tell you I won't be bathed, I won't, I won't!"

There is one contraction in this passage that we haven't talked about: **o'clock**. **O'clock** is a contraction for the phrase **of the clock**.

Copywork

Contractions

Write the contraction for each pair of words.

is not	are not	was not
were not	do not	does not
did not	have not	has not
had not	could not	will not

40. Linking Verbs

- Peter Pan, Chapter 3

Linking means to connect or join. Linking verbs connect a noun or a pronoun with more information about the person, place, thing, or idea. Are you ready to learn the linking verbs?

The linking verbs are am, are, is, was, were, be, being, been, become, seem

Do you recognize these verbs? You should! Most of them are the state of being verbs that you've memorized! State of being verbs only show that someone or something exists. They don't tell us anything else about the noun or pronoun. But we can also use them as linking verbs to say something interesting about the noun or pronoun.

Look at these sentences from *Peter Pan*:

"<u>I am</u> captain."

If Peter Pan just said, "I am," that would not give us much information. Instead, Peter says, "I am <u>captain</u>."

"<u>I am</u> a gentleman and <u>you are</u> a lady."

If Peter Pan just said, "I am and you are," that would not give us much information. Instead, Peter says "I am <u>a gentleman</u> and you are <u>a lady</u>."

<u>It is</u> the fairy language.

Instead of just being told, "It is," we're told, "It is <u>the fairy language</u>."

<u>It was</u> a fairy.

Instead of just being told, "It was," we're told, "It was <u>a fairy</u>."

The Coin
by Sara Teasdale

In to my heart's treasury
I slipped a coin
That time cannot take
Nor a thief purloin,—
Oh, better than the minting
Of a gold-crowned king
Is the safe-kept memory
Of a lovely thing.

The Shepherd and the Lion
An Aesop's Fable

    A Shepherd, counting his Sheep one day, discovered that a number of them were missing.
    Much irritated, he very loudly and boastfully declared that he would catch the thief and punish him as he deserved. The Shepherd suspected a Wolf of the deed and so set out toward a rocky region among the hills, where there were caves infested by Wolves. But before starting out he made a vow to Jupiter that if he would help him find the thief he would offer a fat Calf as a sacrifice.
    The Shepherd searched a long time without finding any Wolves, but just as he was passing near a large cave on the mountain side, a huge Lion stalked out, carrying a Sheep. In great terror the Shepherd fell on his knees.
    "Alas, O Jupiter, man does not know what he asks! To find the thief I offered to sacrifice a fat Calf. Now I promise you a full-grown Bull, if you but make the thief go away!"
    We are often not so eager for what we seek, after we have found it.
    Do not foolishly ask for things that would bring ruin if they were granted.

Exercise

In your workbook, circle each linking verb from this passage:

> He had to translate. "She is not very polite. She says you are a great ugly girl, and that she is my fairy."

Then, look at each linking verb and underline the noun or pronoun and the interesting information that the linking verb connects to it.

Copywork

Literature

> "She is not very polite. She says you are a great ugly girl, and that she is my fairy."

Poetry—Solomon Grundy

> Christened on Tuesday,
> Married on Wednesday,
> Took ill on Thursday,
> Worse on Friday,

41. Linking Verbs

- Peter Pan, Chapter 4

The linking verbs are: am, are, is, was, were, be, being, been, become, seem. When we use state of being verbs, they just tell us that something exists. When we use linking verbs, we use them to connect a noun or a pronoun with more information about the person, place, thing, or idea. Look at these sentences from *Peter Pan*:

"I am Wendy," she said agitatedly.

"He is the worst."

Sometimes it was dark.

They were sleepy.

I'm going to give you a noun and a linking verb. Complete the sentence by saying something interesting about each noun.

I am _____.

You are _____.

Wendy, John, and Michael are _____.

Fairies are _____.

Peter Pan is _____.

Neverland is _____.

Captain Hook was _____.

The Lost Boys were _____.

A Barefoot Boy
by James Whitcomb Riley

A barefoot boy! I mark him at his play —
For May is here once more, and so is he, —
His dusty trousers, rolled half to the knee,
And his bare ankles grimy, too, as they:
Cross-hatchings of the nettle, in array
Of feverish stripes, hint vividly to me

Of woody pathways winding endlessly
Along the creek, where even yesterday
He plunged his shrinking body — gasped and shook —
Yet called the water "warm," with never lack
Of joy. And so, half enviously I look
Upon this graceless barefoot and his track, —
His toe stubbed — ay, his big toe-nail knocked back
Like unto the clasp of an old pocketbook.

The Ant and the Dove
An Aesop's Fable

A Dove saw an Ant fall into a brook. The Ant struggled in vain to reach the bank, and in pity, the Dove dropped a blade of straw close beside it. Clinging to the straw like a shipwrecked sailor to a broken spar, the Ant floated safely to shore.

Soon after, the Ant saw a man getting ready to kill the Dove with a stone. But just as he cast the stone, the Ant stung him in the heel, so that the pain made him miss his aim, and the startled Dove flew to safety in a distant wood.

A kindness is never wasted.

Exercise

In your workbook, circle each linking verb from this passage:

> "That is the awful thing, John. We should have to go on, for we don't know how to stop."
>
> This was true, Peter had forgotten to show them how to stop.

Look at each linking verb and underline the noun or pronoun and the interesting information that the linking verb connects to it.

Copywork

Literature

> "That is the awful thing, John. We should have to go on, for we don't know how to stop."

Maxim

> April showers bring May flowers.

42. Narration: The Fox and the Grapes

- Peter Pan, Chapter 5

It's time for a **narration**. Your instructor will read this fable to you, and you will tell the story back to her while she writes it down for you. Then your instructor will write part of it for you to use as copywork.

The Fox and the Grapes
An Aesop's Fable

A Fox one day spied a beautiful bunch of ripe grapes hanging from a vine trained along the branches of a tree. The grapes seemed ready to burst with juice, and the Fox's mouth watered as he gazed longingly at them.

The bunch hung from a high branch, and the Fox had to jump for it. The first time he jumped he missed it by a long way. So he walked off a short distance and took a running leap at it, only to fall short once more. Again and again he tried, but in vain.

Now he sat down and looked at the grapes in disgust.

"What a fool I am," he said. "Here I am wearing myself out to get a bunch of sour grapes that are not worth gaping for."

And off he walked very, very scornfully.

There are many who pretend to despise and belittle that which is beyond their reach.

Wishing
by William Allingham

Ring ting! I wish I were a Primrose,
A bright yellow Primrose, blowing in the spring!
The stooping bough above me,
The wandering bee to love me,
The fern and moss to creep across,
And the Elm-tree for our king!

Nay,—stay! I wish I were an Elm-tree,
A great lofty Elm-tree, with green leaves gay!
The winds would set them dancing,
The sun and moonshine glance in,
And birds would house among the boughs,
And sweetly sing.

Oh,—no! I wish I were a Robin,—
A Robin, or a little Wren, everywhere to go,
Through forest, field or garden,
And ask no leave or pardon,
Till winter comes with icy thumbs
To ruffle up our wing!

Well,—tell! where should I fly to,
Where to sleep, in the dark wood or dell?
Before the day was over,
Home must come the rover,
For mother's kiss,—sweeter this
Than any other thing.

Copywork

Narration

Instructor: Write or print part of today's narration to use as copywork.

43. Abbreviations: Titles of Respect

- Peter Pan, Chapter 6

Remember that sometimes we use an abbreviation instead of writing out an entire word, like Jan. for January or St. for street. When we use the following titles of respect as part of a person's name, the title of respect is always abbreviated. Since these titles of respect are part of a person's name, they are capitalized.

Mister	Mr.	The title for a man.
Doctor	Dr.	The title for a doctor.
Mistress	Mrs.	The title for a married woman. Although this abbreviation stands for "mistress," we actually pronounce Mrs. as "missuss."

The other two most common titles of respect are a little different. Miss doesn't have an abbreviation at all, and Ms. is only an abbreviation!

Miss	Miss	The title for an unmarried woman.
Ms.	Ms.	This title may be used for either a married or an unmarried woman.

The Arrow and the Song
by Henry Wadsworth Longfellow

I shot an arrow into the air,
It fell to earth, I knew not where;
For, so swiftly it flew, the sight
Could not follow it in its flight.

I breathed a song into the air,
It fell to earth, I knew not where;
For who has sight so keen and strong,
That it can follow the flight of song?

Long, long afterward, in an oak
I found the arrow, still unbroke;
And the song, from beginning to end,
I found again in the heart of a friend.

The Swallow and the Crow
An Aesop's Fable

The Swallow and the Crow had an argument one day about their plumage.

Said the Swallow: "Just look at my bright and downy feathers. Your black stiff quills are not worth having. Why don't you dress better? Show a little pride!"

"Your feathers may do very well in spring," replied the Crow, "but—I don't remember ever having seen you around in winter, and that's when I enjoy myself most."

Friends in fine weather only, are not worth much.

Exercise

In your workbook, write N above each of the nouns and V above each of the verbs from this passage. If a proper noun has more than one word, make arms stretched out to include the whole thing, like this: ———N———

In a tremble they opened the street door. Mr. Darling would have rushed upstairs, but Mrs. Darling signed him to go softly.

Copywork

Literature

Mr. Darling would have rushed upstairs, but Mrs. Darling signed him to go softly.

Poetry—Solomon Grundy

Died on Saturday,
Buried on Sunday.
This is the end
Of Solomon Grundy.

44. Review: Name, Address, and Phone Number

- Peter Pan, Chapter 7

Your address tells people where you live. Your street address is the house number and the name of the street on which you live. Your full address will also include the name of the town or city, the state, and your zip code.

When we write all of this information on an envelope to mail to a person, then the post office is able to deliver the letter.

How many people live in your home? Most people live in a house with other people, so when we address an envelope, we must also write the name of the person to whom the letter is written. We usually write both the first name and the last name, and we can also include a title of respect like Mr., Dr., Mrs., Miss, or Ms. Today you'll be writing your name and address. This is the information that a person would need to write on an envelope to mail a letter to you!

Remember that your phone number is ten digits long. Do you remember what the first three digits are called? The first three digits are your area code. They are the same for everyone in your area of the country. The last seven digits are unique—no one else in your area code can have those exact seven digits in exactly that order.

For your copywork today, write your name, address, and phone number. Have you memorized it so that you can do it from memory? If you haven't, or if you have trouble spelling some of the words, ask your instructor to write it for you to copy.

The Ruin
by Walter de la Mare

When the last colors of the day
Have from their burning ebbed away,
About that ruin, cold and lone,
The cricket shrills from stone to stone;
And scattering o'er its darkened green,
Bands of the fairies may be seen,
Chattering like grasshoppers, their feet

Dancing a thistledown dance round it:
While the great gold of the mild moon
Tinges their tiny acorn shoon.

Jupiter and the Monkey
An Aesop's Fable

There was once a baby show among the Animals in the forest. Jupiter provided the prize. Of course all the proud mammas from far and near brought their babies. But none got there earlier than Mother Monkey. Proudly she presented her baby among the other contestants.

As you can imagine, there was quite a laugh when the Animals saw the ugly flat-nosed, hairless, pop-eyed little creature.

"Laugh if you will," said the Mother Monkey. "Though Jupiter may not give him the prize, I know that he is the prettiest, the sweetest, the dearest darling in the world."

Mother love is blind.

Exercise

In your workbook, underline the pronouns from this passage:

> When she sat down to a basketful of their stockings, every heel with a hole in it, she would fling up her arms and exclaim, "Oh dear, I am sure I sometimes think spinsters are to be envied!"

What is the antecedent (the noun being replaced) of each pronoun?

Copywork

Name, Address, and Phone Number

> Instructor: Have the child write his name, address, and phone number, or write it for him to copy.

Bible—James 5:13

> Is anyone among you suffering? Then he must pray. Is anyone cheerful? He is to sing praises.

Girl Carrying a Basket by Winslow Homer

Picture Study

1. Read the title and the name of the artist. Study the picture for several minutes, then put the picture away.

2. Describe the picture.

3. Look at the picture again. Do you notice any details that you missed before? What do you like or dislike about this painting? Does it remind you of anything?

45. Quotations: Review, Punctuation; Picture Study: Girl Carrying a Basket

- Peter Pan, Chapter 8

Do you remember learning about direct and indirect quotations? Direct quotations tell us exactly what someone said. Indirect quotations tell us what someone said but without using the person's exact words. Look at this sentence from *Peter Pan*:

"Captain, is all well?" they asked timidly.

This is a direct quotation because it tells us the exact words that they said. Can you change that direct quotation to an indirect quotation? Here's one way:

They asked the captain if all was well.

This indirect quotation gives us the same information as the direct quotation, but it doesn't use the exact words that were spoken.

Now let's look at the punctuation in the following sentence:

"Set her free," came the astonishing answer.

We place quotation marks around the direct quotation to show the exact words spoken, and we also use a comma between the direct quotation and the rest of the sentence. The comma is inside the quotation marks.

An Evening Hymn
by Thomas Ken

All praise to thee, my God, this night,
For all the blessings of the light;
Keep me, O keep me, King of Kings,
Beneath thy own almighty wings.

Forgive me, Lord, for thy dear Son,
The ill that I this day have done;
That with the world, myself, and Thee,
I, ere I sleep, at peace may be.

O may my soul on Thee repose,
And may sweet sleep my eyelids close:
Sleep that may me more vigorous make
To serve my God when I awake.

Exercise

In your workbook, there are three direct quotations from *Peter Pan*, but there are no quotation marks! Can you add the missing punctuation marks to the sentences?

He sighs   said Smee.

He sighs again   said Starkey.

And yet a third time he sighs   said Smee.

Copywork

Literature

"We are on the rock, Wendy," he said, "but it is growing smaller. Soon the water will be over it."

46. Definition: Conjunction

- Peter Pan, Chapter 9

A conjunction is a word that joins words or groups of words together.

Conjunctions are special words that help us to join words or groups of words together. There are many conjunctions, but we're only going to learn about the three most common conjunctions right now: and, but, or.

> Chickens are birds. Ducks are birds.
> Chickens <u>and</u> ducks are birds.

In this sentence, the word **and** joins the nouns **chickens** and **ducks**. We can also join two action verbs together with **and**:

> The children skipped. The children hopped.
> The children skipped <u>and</u> hopped.

Make a sentence using the conjunction **and**. Think about two things you like to do, two animals you like, or two foods you like to eat.

> You can play <u>or</u> read until bedtime.

We use the conjunction **or** to join words when we must choose. You can't play and read at the same time, so you must choose one or the other! Make a sentence using the conjunction **or**.

> The boy played, <u>but</u> his sister did not.
>
> I want to read, <u>but</u> I can't find my book.

In these sentences, we joined groups of words. In the first, we joined **the boy played** with **his sister did not**. Which groups of words did we join in the second sentence? Now, make a sentence using the conjunction **but**.

Which conjunctions (and, but, or) are missing from these sentences?

Wendy _____ her brothers went to Neverland.

In Neverland, the children played _____ had adventures.

They could stay in Neverland _____ they could go home.

They wanted to stay in Neverland, _____ their parents missed them.

Carol
by William Canton

When the herds were watching
In the midnight chill,
Came a spotless lambkin
From the heavenly hill.

Snow was on the mountains,
And the wind was cold,
When from God's own garden
Dropped a rose of gold.

When 'twas bitter winter,
Houseless and forlorn
In a star-lit stable
Christ the Babe was born.

Welcome, heavenly lambkin;
Welcome, golden rose;
Alleluia, Baby,
In the swaddling clothes!

The Hare and His Ears
An Aesop's Fable

The Lion had been badly hurt by the horns of a Goat, which he was eating. He was very angry to think that any animal that he chose for a meal, should be so brazen as to wear such dangerous things as horns to scratch him while he ate. So he commanded that all animals with horns should leave his domains within twenty-four hours.

The command struck terror among the beasts. All those who were so unfortunate as to have horns, began to pack up and move out. Even the Hare, who, as you know, has no horns and so had nothing to fear, passed a very restless night, dreaming awful dreams about the fearful Lion.

And when he came out of the warren in the early morning sunshine, and there saw the shadow cast by his long and pointed ears, a terrible fright seized him.

"Goodby, neighbor Cricket," he called. "I'm off. He will certainly make out that my ears are horns, no matter what I say."

Do not give your enemies the slightest reason to attack your reputation.

Your enemies will seize any excuse to attack you.

Exercise

In your workbook, underline the conjunction from this passage:

Well, not only could they not understand each other, but they forgot their manners.

Which words or groups of words are being joined by the conjunction?

Copywork

Literature

Well, not only could they not understand each other, but they forgot their manners.

Poetry—Carol

When the herds were watching
In the midnight chill,
Came a spotless lambkin
From the heavenly hill.

47. Helping Verbs

- Peter Pan, Chapter 10

Do you ever need help to do something? Sometimes, verbs need help, too! Read these sentences from *Peter Pan*:

"Slightly ___ coughing on the table."

"Nibs ___ speaking with his mouth full."

"I ___ spoken."

In the sentences above, I took out the helping verbs. They sound funny, don't they? Now read them with the helping verbs:

"Slightly <u>is</u> coughing on the table."

"Nibs <u>is</u> speaking with his mouth full."

"I <u>have</u> spoken."

The helping verbs are:

am, are, is,	was, were,	be, being, been,
do, does, did,	have, has, had,	may, might, must,
can, could,	shall, should,	will, would

Look at the first line of helping verbs. You already know those! They are the state of being verbs. They can act as linking verbs or helping verbs. We call them state of being verbs when they just show that something exists, linking verbs when they link words together, and helping verbs when they help other verbs.

You should memorize the entire list so that you will recognize them in a sentence. A helping verb is part of the verb, so when you label verbs in a sentence, underline the entire verb and write the V above it.

——V——

"My old bones <u>would rattle</u>!"

——V——

"I <u>must have</u> somebody in a cradle."

A Cradle Song
by William Blake

Sweet dreams, form a shade
O'er my lovely infant's head!
Sweet dreams of pleasant streams
By happy, silent, moony beams!

Sweet Sleep, with soft down
Weave thy brows an infant crown!
Sweet Sleep, angel mild,
Hover o'er my happy child!

Sweet smiles, in the night
Hover over my delight!
Sweet smiles, mother's smiles,
All the livelong night beguiles.

Sweet moans, dovelike sighs,
Chase not slumber from thy eyes!
Sweet moans, sweeter smiles,
All the dovelike moans beguiles.

Sleep, sleep, happy child!
All creation slept and smiled.
Sleep, sleep, happy sleep,
While o'er thee thy mother weep.

Sweet babe, in thy face
Holy image I can trace;
Sweet babe, once like thee
Thy Maker lay, and wept for me:

Wept for me, for thee, for all,
When He was an infant small.
Thou His image ever see,
Heavenly face that smiles on thee!

Smiles on thee, on me, on all,
Who became an infant small;
Infant smiles are His own smiles;
Heaven and earth to peace beguiles.

The Mole and His Mother
An Aesop's Fable

    A little Mole once said to his Mother:
    "Why, Mother, you said I was blind! But I am sure I can see!"
    Mother Mole saw she would have to get such conceit out of his head. So she put a bit of frankincense before him and asked him to tell what it was.

The little Mole peered at it.

"Why, that's a pebble!"

"Well, my son, that proves you've lost your sense of smell as well as being blind."

Boast of one thing and you will be found lacking in that and a few other things as well.

Exercise

In your workbook, underline the verbs from this passage:

> "Oh yes, Tinker Bell will tell you," Wendy retorted scornfully. "She is an abandoned little creature."

Label the action verbs V and the linking verbs LV. Be careful not to forget the helping verbs! Make arms stretched out to include the whole thing, like this: ———V———

Copywork

Literature

> "Oh yes, Tinker Bell will tell you," Wendy retorted scornfully. "She is an abandoned little creature."

Maxim

> Charity begins at home.

48. Narration: The Farmer and His Sons

- Peter Pan, Chapter 11

It's time for a narration. Your instructor will read this fable to you, and you will tell the story back to her while she writes it down for you. Then your instructor will write part of it for you to use as copywork.

The Farmer and His Sons
An Aesop's Fable

A rich old farmer, who felt that he had not many more days to live, called his sons to his bedside.

"My sons," he said, "heed what I have to say to you. Do not on any account part with the estate that has belonged to our family for so many generations. Somewhere on it is hidden a rich treasure. I do not know the exact spot, but it is there, and you will surely find it. Spare no energy and leave no spot unturned in your search."

The father died, and no sooner was he in his grave than the sons set to work digging with all their might, turning up every foot of ground with their spades, and going over the whole farm two or three times.

No hidden gold did they find; but at harvest time when they had settled their accounts and had pocketed a rich profit far greater than that of any of their neighbors, they understood that the treasure their father had told them about was the wealth of a bountiful crop, and that in their industry had they found the treasure.

Industry is itself a treasure.

The Song of the Soldiers
by Walter de la Mare

As I sat musing by the frozen dyke,
There was a man marching with a bright steel pike,
Marching in the dayshine like a ghost came he,
And behind me was the moaning and the murmur
    Of the sea.

As I sat musing, 'twas not one but ten —-
Rank on rank of ghostly soldiers marching o'er the fen,
Marching in the misty air they showed in dreams to me,

And behind me was the shouting and the shattering
    Of the sea.

As I sat musing, 'twas a host in dark array,
With their horses and their cannon wheeling onward to the fray,
Moving like a shadow to the fate the brave must dree,
And behind me roared the drums, rang the trumpets
    Of the sea.

Copywork

Narration

Instructor: Write or print part of today's narration to use as copywork.

49. Linking Verbs and Helping Verbs

- Peter Pan, Chapter 12

The helping verbs are:

    am, are, is,   was, were,   be, being, been,
    do, does, did,   have, has, had,   may, might, must,
    can, could,   shall, should,   will, would

Remember that am, are, is, was, were, be, being, and been can be either linking verbs or helping verbs. Look at the word **was** in the following sentences from *Peter Pan*:

    It was Peter's cockiness.

    It was Pan he wanted.

In these sentences, **was** is a linking verb. In the first sentence, **was** links **it** to **Peter's cockiness**. In the second sentence, **was** links **it** to **Pan**. Now look at this sentence:

    The air was torn with the war-cry; but it was now too late.

The word **was** appears twice in this sentence. Which one is a helping verb, and which one is a linking verb?

The first **was** is a helping verb. It is helping the action verb **torn**. The second **was** is a linking verb. It is linking **it** with **too late**.

Sometimes, an action verb may need more than one helping verb. In the following sentence, **would** and **have** are both helping the action verb **made**.

    On the other hand, this would have made his strategy of no avail.

Sometimes, a word will be between the action verb and its helper. When that happens, you can label the helping verb HV.

        HV   V
"You will never hear the tom-tom again," he muttered.

The Midden's Song
by Walter de la Mare

"Bubble, Bubble,
   Swim to see
Oh, how beautiful
   I be.

"Fishes, Fishes,
   Finned and fine,
What's your gold
   Compared with mine?

"Why, then, has
   Wise Tishnar made
One so lovely,
   Yet so sad?

"Lone am I,
   And can but make
A little song,
   For singing's sake."

The Wolves and the Sheep
An Aesop's Fable

    A pack of Wolves lurked near the Sheep pasture. But the Dogs kept them all at a respectful distance, and the Sheep grazed in perfect safety. But now the Wolves thought of a plan to trick the Sheep.
    "Why is there always this hostility between us?" they said. "If it were not for those Dogs who are always stirring up trouble, I am sure we should get along beautifully. Send them away and you will see what good friends we shall become."
    The Sheep were easily fooled. They persuaded the Dogs to go away, and that very evening the Wolves had the grandest feast of their lives.
    Do not give up friends for foes.
    Exercise
    In your workbook, underline the verbs from this passage:
    Every foot of ground between the spot where Hook had landed his forces and the home under the trees was stealthily examined.
    There are two action verbs, and both of them have helping verbs. Look carefully. The second one is rather stealthy!

Copywork

Literature

    Every foot of ground between the spot where Hook had landed his forces and the home under the trees was stealthily examined.

Poetry—Carol

Snow was on the mountains,
And the wind was cold,
When from God's own garden
Dropped a rose of gold.

50. Quotations: Punctuation

- Peter Pan, Chapter 13

We use quotation marks to show a direct quotation, the exact words that someone spoke. Look at this sentence from *Peter Pan*:

"I won't open unless you speak," Peter cried.

We place quotation marks around the direct quotation to show the exact words spoken, and we also use a comma between the direct quotation and the rest of the sentence. Notice that the comma at the end of the direct quotation is inside the quotation marks.

Sometimes, a direct quotation ends with a question mark or an exclamation mark. When that happens, we don't add the comma. We just place the ending quotation mark after the question mark or the exclamation mark, like this:

"Oh, you could never guess!" she cried, and offered him three guesses.

"What is the matter with you?" cried Peter, suddenly afraid.

Look at your copywork sentence for today. Is it a direct quotation or an indirect quotation? Why? Can you change it to the other type of quotation?

In the Train
by Sara Teasdale

Fields beneath a quilt of snow
From which the rocks and stubble sleep,
And in the west a shy white star
That shivers as it wakes from deep.

The restless rumble of the train,
The drowsy people in the car,
Steel blue twilight in the world,
And in my heart a timid star.

The Cock and the Fox
An Aesop's Fable

A Fox was caught in a trap one fine morning, because he had got too near the Farmer's hen house. No doubt he was hungry, but that was not an excuse for stealing. A Cock, rising early, discovered what had happened. He knew the Fox could not get at him, so he went a little closer to get a good look at his enemy.

The Fox saw a slender chance of escape. "Dear friend," he said, "I was just on my way to visit a sick relative, when I stumbled into this string and got all tangled up. But please do not tell anybody about it. I dislike causing sorrow to anybody, and I am sure I can soon gnaw this string to pieces."

But the Cock was not to be so easily fooled. He soon roused the whole hen yard, and when the Farmer came running out, that was the end of Mr. Fox.

The wicked deserve no aid.

Exercise

In your workbook, there are two direct quotations, but the punctuation marks are missing again! Can you add the missing punctuation marks to the sentences? First, you will have to decide whether each direct quotation needs a question mark or an exclamation mark. Here's the passage:

Do you believe   he cried.

What do you think   she asked Peter.

Copywork

Literature

She was saying that she thought she could get well again if children believed in fairies.

Bible—Proverbs 15:1

A gentle answer turns away wrath,
But a harsh word stirs up anger.

On the Fence by Winslow Homer

Picture Study

1. Read the title and the name of the artist. Study the picture for several minutes, then put the picture away.

2. Describe the picture.

3. Look at the picture again. Do you notice any details that you missed before? What do you like or dislike about this painting? Does it remind you of anything?

51. Helping Verbs; Picture Study: On the Fence

- Peter Pan, Chapter 14

The helping verbs are:

    am, are, is,   was, were,   be, being, been,
    do, does, did,   have, has, had,   may, might, must,
    can, could,   shall, should,   will, would

Can you find the helping verbs in this sentence from *Peter Pan*? Which action verbs do they help?

> She was wrapped in the blanket of night, through which no sound from her could have reached the shore.

The helping verb **was** helps the verb **wrapped**. The helping verbs **could have** help the verb **reached**.

Remember, sometimes helping verbs are separated from the verbs that they are helping. Find the helping verbs in these sentences from *Peter Pan*. Which verbs do they help?

> But as those who read between the lines must already have guessed, he had been at a famous public school.

In the above sentence, **must have** helps **guessed**. The other helping verb isn't helping an action verb. **Had** helps the state of being verb **been**.

November
by Alice Cary

The leaves are fading and falling,
The winds are rough and wild,
The birds have ceased their calling,
But let me tell you, my child,
Though day by day, as it closes,

Doth darker and colder grow,
The roots of the bright red roses
Will keep alive in the snow.
And when the Winter is over,
The boughs will get new leaves,
The quail come back to the clover,
And the swallow back to the eaves.
The robin will wear on his bosom
A vest that is bright and new,
And the loveliest way-side blossom
Will shine with the sun and dew.
The leaves to-day are whirling,
The brooks are dry and dumb,
But let me tell you, my darling,
The Spring will be sure to come.
There must be rough, cold weather,
And winds and rains so wild;
Not all good things together
Come to us here, my child.
So, when some dear joy loses
Its beauteous summer glow,
Think how the roots of the roses
Are kept alive in the snow.

Exercise

In your workbook, underline the verbs from this passage:

> She was wrapped in the blanket of night, through which no sound from her could have reached the shore.

Which words are the helping verbs? Which action verbs do they help? Hint: There are two action verbs, and both of them have helping verbs.

Copywork

Literature

> She was wrapped in the blanket of night, through which no sound from her could have reached the shore.

52. Letter from Neverland

- Peter Pan, Chapter 15

Wendy, John, and Michael have been away from home for quite a long while now, and they're still not ready to go home! Will you help so that Mr. and Mrs. Darling can stop worrying?

Pretend to be Wendy, John, or Michael and write a letter home to No. 14. Maybe we can convince Tinker Bell to deliver it. Maybe. Here's how to write your letter.

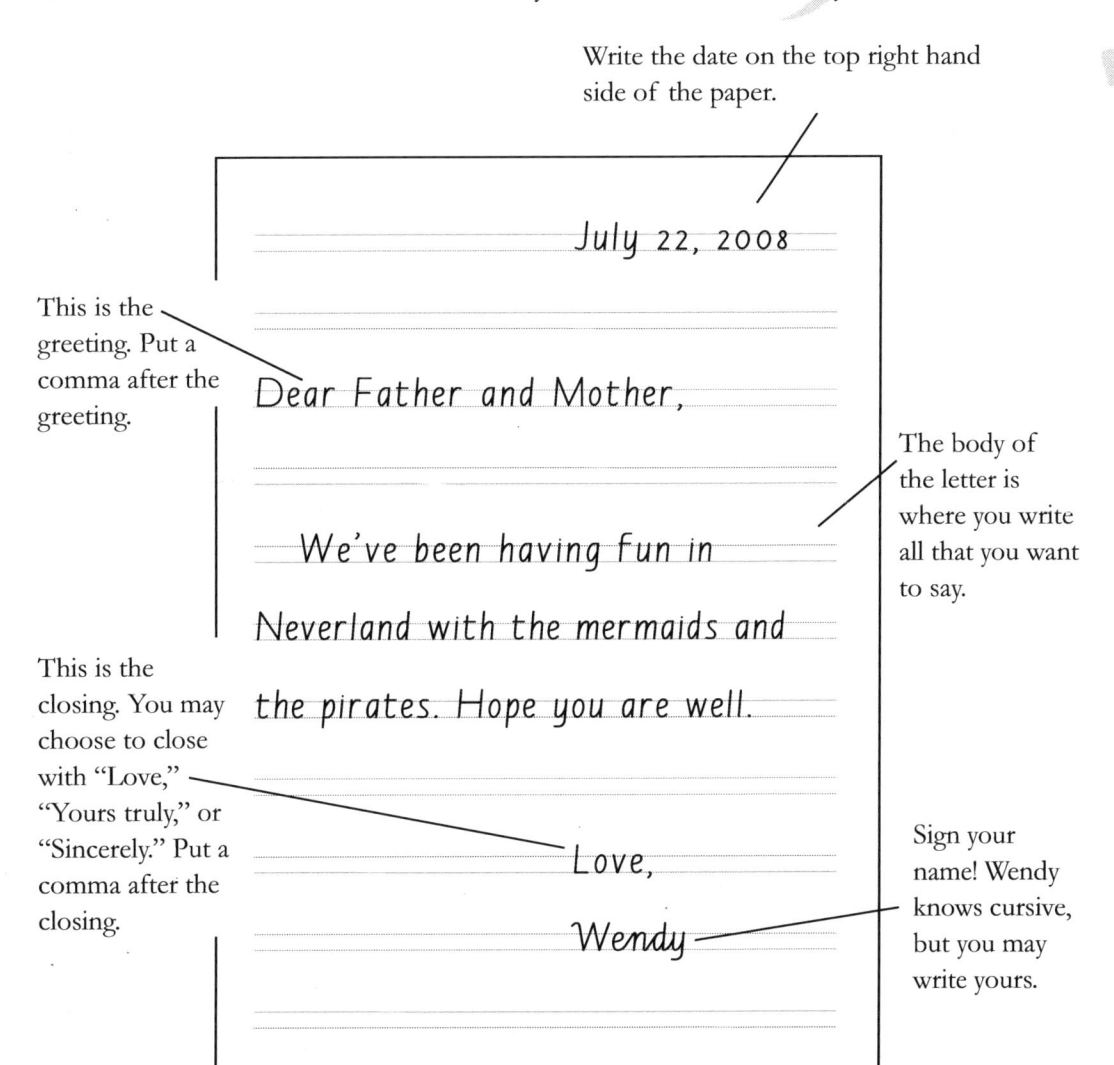

Write the date on the top right hand side of the paper.

> July 22, 2008
>
> Dear Father and Mother,
>
> We've been having fun in Neverland with the mermaids and the pirates. Hope you are well.
>
> Love,
> Wendy

This is the greeting. Put a comma after the greeting.

The body of the letter is where you write all that you want to say.

This is the closing. You may choose to close with "Love," "Yours truly," or "Sincerely." Put a comma after the closing.

Sign your name! Wendy knows cursive, but you may write yours.

The Ass in the Lion's Skin
An Aesop's Fable

An Ass found a Lion's skin left in the forest by a hunter. He dressed himself in it, and amused himself by hiding in a thicket and rushing out suddenly at the animals who passed that way. All took to their heels the moment they saw him.

The Ass was so pleased to see the animals running away from him, just as if he were King Lion himself, that he could not keep from expressing his delight by a loud, harsh bray. A Fox, who ran with the rest, stopped short as soon as he heard the voice. Approaching the Ass, he said with a laugh:

"If you had kept your mouth shut you might have frightened me, too. But you gave yourself away with that silly bray."

A fool may deceive by his dress and appearance, but his words will soon show what he really is.

Exercise

In your workbook, write your letter from Neverland.

[Note to instructor: This is a creative writing assignment. Many young children have difficulty with creative writing assignments. If your child feels that this assignment is stressful rather than fun, please either skip the letter or offer plenty of help.]

Copywork

Poetry—Carol

>When 'twas bitter winter,
>Houseless and forlorn
>In a starlit stable
>Christ the Babe was born.

The Fairies
by William Allingham

Up the airy mountain
Down the rushy glen,
We daren't go a-hunting,
For fear of little men;
Wee folk, good folk,
Trooping all together;
Green jacket, red cap,
And white owl's feather.
Down along the rocky shore
Some make their home,
They live on crispy pancakes
Of yellow tide-foam;
Some in the reeds
Of the black mountain-lake,
With frogs for their watch-dogs,
All night awake.

High on the hill-top
The old King sits;
He is now so old and gray
He's nigh lost his wits.
With a bridge of white mist
Columbkill he crosses,
On his stately journeys
From Slieveleague to Rosses;
Or going up with music,
On cold starry nights,
To sup with the Queen,
Of the gay Northern Lights.

They stole little Bridget
For seven years long;
When she came down again
Her friends were all gone.
They took her lightly back
Between the night and morrow;
They thought she was fast asleep,
But she was dead with sorrow.
They have kept her ever since
Deep within the lake,
On a bed of flag leaves,
Watching till she wake.

By the craggy hill-side,
Through the mosses bare,
They have planted thorn trees
For pleasure here and there.
Is any man so daring
As dig them up in spite?
He shall find the thornies set
In his bed at night.

Up the airy mountain
Down the rushy glen,
We daren't go a-hunting,
For fear of little men;
Wee folk, good folk,
Trooping all together;
Green jacket, red cap,
And white owl's feather.

53. Addressing an Envelope

• Peter Pan, Chapter 16

Below, you can see an example of how to address an envelope. The Darlings' address is not complete since there is no street name or zip code. However, it's being sent by Neverland Fairy Mail, and fairies are not as particular about these things as the Post Office.

The return address is the address of the person who is sending the letter. We write it in the top left corner.

We place the stamp in the top right corner.

Wendy Moira Angela Darling
The House Under the Ground
Neverland

Mr. and Mrs. Darling
No. 14
London

This is where we write the address of the person who will be receiving the letter.

A Winter Blue Jay
by Sara Teasdale

Crisply the bright snow whispered,
Crunching beneath our feet;
Behind us as we walked along the parkway,
Our shadows danced,
Fantastic shapes in vivid blue.
Across the lake the skaters
Flew to and fro,
With sharp turns weaving
A frail invisible net.
In ecstasy the earth
Drank the silver sunlight;
In ecstasy the skaters
Drank the wine of speed;
In ecstasy we laughed
Drinking the wine of love.
Had not the music of our joy
Sounded its highest note?
But no,

For suddenly, with lifted eyes you said,
"Oh look!"
There, on the black bough of a snow flecked maple,
Fearless and gay as our love,
A blue jay cocked his crest!
Oh who can tell the range of joy
Or set the bounds of beauty?

The Fisherman and the Little Fish
An Aesop's Fable

    A poor Fisherman, who lived on the fish he caught, had bad luck one day and caught nothing but a very small fry. The Fisherman was about to put it in his basket when the little Fish said:
    "Please spare me, Mr. Fisherman! I am so small it is not worth while to carry me home. When I am bigger, I shall make you a much better meal."
    But the Fisherman quickly put the fish into his basket.
    "How foolish I should be," he said, "to throw you back. However small you may be, you are better than nothing at all."
    A small gain is worth more than a large promise.

Exercise

In your workbook, label the nouns N and the verbs V from this passage:

    "John," he said, looking around him doubtfully, "I think I have been here before."

Copywork

Literature

"John," he said, looking around him doubtfully, "I think I have been here before."

Maxim

Where there is a will there is a way.

54. Narration: The Ants and the Grasshopper

- Peter Pan, Chapter 17

It's time for a narration. Your instructor will read this fable to you, and you will tell the story back to her while she writes it down for you. Then your instructor will write part of it for you to use as copywork.

The Ants and the Grasshopper
An Aesop's Fable

One bright day in late autumn a family of Ants were bustling about in the warm sunshine, drying out the grain they had stored up during the summer, when a starving Grasshopper, his fiddle under his arm, came up and humbly begged for a bite to eat.

"What!" cried the Ants in surprise, "haven't you stored anything away for the winter? What in the world were you doing all last summer?"

"I didn't have time to store up any food," whined the Grasshopper. "I was so busy making music that before I knew it the summer was gone."

The Ants shrugged their shoulders in disgust.

"Making music, were you?" they cried. "Very well; now dance!" And they turned their backs on the Grasshopper and went on with their work.

There's a time for work and a time for play.

The Cricket and the Ant
Anonymous, adapted from Aesop

A silly young cricket accustomed to sing
Through the warm sunny months of gay summer and spring,
Began to complain, when he found that at home
His cupboard was empty,
And winter was come.

Not a crumb to be found
On the snow-covered ground;
Not a flower could he see,
Not a leaf on the tree;
"Oh, what will become," says the cricket, "of me?"

At last, by starvation and famine made bold,
All dripping with wet, and all trembling with cold,
Away he set off to a miserly ant,
To see if, to keep him alive, he would grant
Him shelter from rain,
And a mouthful of grain.
He wished only to borrow,
He'd repay it to-morrow:
If not, he must die of starvation and sorrow.

Says the ant to the cricket, "I'm your servant and friend,
But we ants never borrow; we ants never lend.
But tell me, dear cricket, did you lay nothing by
When the weather was warm?" Quoth the cricket, "Not I!
My heart was so light
That I sang day and night,
For all nature looked gay."
"You sang, sir, you say?
Go, then," says the ant, "and dance winter away!"

Thus ending, he hastily lifted the wicket,
And out of the door turned the poor little cricket.
Folks call this a fable. I'll warrant it true:
Some crickets have four legs, and some have but two.

Copywork

Narration

> Instructor: Write or print part of today's narration to use as copywork.

55. Definition: Sentence; Declarative Sentences

- The Wind in the Willows, Chapter 1

**A sentence is a group of words
that expresses a complete thought.**

A sentence begins with a capital letter and ends with a punctuation mark, and it must express a complete thought. Any group of words can begin with a capital letter and end with a punctuation mark, but if it doesn't express a complete thought, it is only a fragment. Fragment means a piece, so a fragment is only a piece of a sentence. Look at these examples:

The birds swooped and soared.

The birds.

The first is a sentence. It expresses a complete thought by telling us what the birds did. The second is only a fragment.

Look at these examples. Can you tell the fragment from the sentence?

Flying purple people eaters descended upon the city.
Descended upon the city.

The first is a sentence because it expresses a complete thought. The second is only a fragment.

There are four types of sentences, and we're going to talk about declarative sentences first. If you announce, "I declare myself to be the ruler of this household," you have given information to your family. (Please note: I do not suggest making such a declaration as it would probably annoy your parents.)

A declarative sentence makes a statement. Its purpose is to give information, and it ends with a period.

The Fighting Cocks and the Eagle
An Aesop's Fable

Once there were two Cocks living in the same farmyard who could not bear the sight of each other. At last one day they flew up to fight it out, beak and claw. They fought until one of them was beaten and crawled off to a corner to hide.

The Cock that had won the battle flew to the top of the hen-house, and, proudly flapping his wings, crowed with all his might to tell the world about his victory. But an Eagle, circling overhead, heard the boasting chanticleer and, swooping down, carried him off to his nest.

His rival saw the deed, and coming out of his corner, took his place as master of the farmyard.

Pride goes before a fall.

Exercise

In your workbook, circle the capital letter that begins each sentence and the period that ends each sentence, and write LV above the linking verb from this passage:

> It was too late. The boat struck the bank full tilt. The dreamer, the joyous oarsman, lay on his back at the bottom of the boat, his heels in the air.

Copywork

Literature

> The dreamer, the joyous oarsman, lay on his back at the bottom of the boat, his heels in the air.

Poetry—Carol

> Welcome, heavenly lambkin;
> Welcome, golden rose;
> Alleluia, Baby,
> In the swaddling clothes!

Night
by William Blake

The sun descending in the West,
The evening star does shine;
The birds are silent in their nest,
And I must seek for mine.
The moon, like a flower
In heaven's high bower,
With silent delight,
Sits and smiles on the night.

Farewell, green fields and happy groves,
Where flocks have took delight,
Where lambs have nibbled, silent moves
The feet of angels bright;
Unseen, they pour blessing,
And joy without ceasing,
On each bud and blossom,
And each sleeping bosom.

They look in every thoughtless nest
Where birds are covered warm;
They visit caves of every beast,
To keep them all from harm:
If they see any weeping
That should have been sleeping,
They pour sleep on their head,
And sit down by their bed.

When wolves and tigers howl for prey,
They pitying stand and weep;
Seeking to drive their thirst away,
And keep them from the sheep.
But, if they rush dreadful,
The angels, most heedful,
Receive each mild spirit,
New worlds to inherit.

And there the lion's ruddy eyes
Shall flow with tears of gold:
And pitying the tender cries,
And walking round the fold:
Saying: 'Wrath by His meekness,
And, by His health, sickness,
Is driven away
From our immortal day.

'And now beside thee, bleating lamb,
I can lie down and sleep,
Or think on Him who bore thy name,
Graze after thee, and weep.
For, washed in life's river,
My bright mane for ever
Shall shine like the gold,
As I guard o'er the fold.'

56. Definition: Adjective

- The Wind in the Willows, Chapter 2

An adjective is a word that modifies a noun or a pronoun.

A noun is the name of a person, place, thing, or idea. **Bird** is a noun. If someone told you that he saw a bird, you might want to know more about the bird. Was it a large bird or a small bird? What color was it? Adjectives tell us more about nouns and pronouns by modifying, or describing, them.

Soft, hard, funny, nice, short, tall, green, furry, cold, hot, wet, sweet.

All of the above words are adjectives. We use them to tell us more about nouns. Can you think of a noun that could be described by each of the adjectives above?

Look at these sentences from *The Wind in the Willows*:

They disembarked, and strolled across the <u>gay</u> <u>flower-decked</u> lawns in search of Toad, whom they presently happened upon resting in a <u>wicker</u> <u>garden</u> chair, with a <u>preoccupied</u> expression of face, and a <u>large</u> map spread out on his knees.

Gay and **flower-decked** describe the lawns. **Gay** means happy, and **flower-decked** tells us that the lawns were not just grass, but that there were flowers there as well. **Wicker** and **garden** describe Toad's chair. It was not a wooden chair nor a metal chair, but wicker! It was not a dining chair nor a reading chair, but a garden chair! **Preoccupied** describes the expression on Toad's face. His expression was neither smiling nor scowling, but preoccupied. And **large** describes the map.

Nouns only name a person, place, thing, or idea. Adjectives describe the person, place, thing, or idea. They help us to picture exactly how the scene appeared to Mole and Rat.

Ducks' Ditty
by Kenneth Grahame

All along the backwater,
Through the rushes tall,
Ducks are a-dabbling,
Up tails all!

Ducks' tails, drakes' tails,
Yellow feet a-quiver,
Yellow bills all out of sight
Busy in the river!

Slushy green undergrowth
Where the roach swim—
Here we keep our larder,
Cool and full and dim.

Every on for what he likes!
We like to be
Heads down, tails up,
Dabbling free!

High in the blue above,
Swifts whirl and call—
We are down a-dabbling
Up tails all!

The Boy and the Nettle
An Aesop's Fable

A Boy, stung by a Nettle, ran home crying, to get his mother to blow on the hurt and kiss it.

"Son," said the Boy's mother, when she had comforted him, "the next time you come near a Nettle, grasp it firmly, and it will be as soft as silk."

Whatever you do, do with all your might.

Exercise

In your workbook, label each noun N and underline the adjectives from this stanza of the Water Rat's poem, "Ducks' Ditty":

Slushy green undergrowth
Where the roach swim—
Here we keep our larder,
Cool and full and dim.

Which noun or pronoun does each adjective describe? Read the rest of the poem again, printed in this lesson. Can you find more adjectives?

Copywork

Literature

Slushy green undergrowth
Where the roach swim—
Here we keep our larder,
Cool and full and dim.

Bible—Matthew 6:9-13, The Lord's Prayer (1 of 3)

Our Father who is in heaven,
Hallowed be Your name.
Your kingdom come.
Your will be done,

Snap the Whip by Winslow Homer

Picture Study

1. Read the title and the name of the artist. Study the picture for several minutes, then put the picture away.

2. Describe the picture.

3. Look at the picture again. Do you notice any details that you missed before? What do you like or dislike about this painting? Does it remind you of anything?

57. Interrogative Sentences; Picture Study: Snap the Whip

- The Wind in the Willows, Chapter 3

A sentence is a group of words that expresses a complete thought.

A sentence begins with a capital letter and ends with a punctuation mark, and it must express a complete thought.

There are four types of sentences. You've already learned that a declarative sentence makes a statement. Its purpose is to give information, and it ends with a period. Today, you will learn about interrogative sentences.

Do you know what the word **interrogate** means? Police may interrogate a person suspected of committing a crime. Your mom may interrogate you and your siblings about who forgot to close the door. **Interrogate** means to ask questions. Now, can you guess what an interrogative sentence does?

An interrogative sentence asks a question. It ends with a question mark. Here are some questions asked in *The Wind in the Willows*:

"Couldn't you ask him here—dinner or something?"

"Where are you? It's me—it's old Rat!"

"Ratty! Is that really you?"

Wanderers
by Walter de la Mare

Wide are the meadows of night,
And daisies are shining there,
Tossing their lovely dews,
Lustrous and fair;
And through these sweet fields go,
Wanderers amid the stars —

Venus, Mercury, Uranus, Neptune,
Saturn, Jupiter, Mars.

'Tired in their silver, they move,
And circling, whisper and say,
Fair are the blossoming meads of delight
Through which we stray.

Exercise

In your workbook, circle the capital letter that begins each sentence and the question mark that ends each interrogative sentence from this passage:

> "Can we eat a doormat? Can we sleep under a doormat? Can we sit on a doormat and sledge home over the snow on it, you exasperating rodent?"

Copywork

Literature

> "Can we sit on a doormat and sledge home over the snow on it, you exasperating rodent?"

58. Exclamatory Sentences

- The Wind in the Willows, Chapter 4

A sentence is a group of words that expresses a complete thought.

An exclamatory sentence expresses sudden or strong feeling. It ends with an exclamation mark.

Like a declarative sentence, an exclamatory sentence can give information, but the exclamation mark tells us that strong or sudden feelings are involved. Look at these sentences from *The Wind in the Willows*, and notice the strong feelings expressed, like surprise or astonishment:

> "What, Ratty, my dear little man!" exclaimed the Badger, in quite a different voice.

Happiness or contentment:

> "No, up and out of doors is good enough to roam about and get one's living in; but underground to come back to at last—that's my idea of home!"

Determination:

> "Any friend of mine walks where he likes in this country, or I'll know the reason why!"

Can you give some examples? What sentence might you exclaim if your mother were baking a cake? If you won a game? If your dog ran off with your favorite toy?

The Flowers
by Robert Louis Stevenson

All the names I know from nurse:
Gardener's garters, Shepherd's purse,

Bachelor's buttons, Lady's smock,
And the Lady Hollyhock.

Fairy places, fairy things,
Fairy woods where the wild bee wings,
Tiny trees for tiny dames—
These must all be fairy names!

Tiny woods below whose boughs
Shady fairies weave a house;
Tiny tree-tops, rose or thyme,
Where the braver fairies climb!

Fair are grown-up people's trees,
But the fairest woods are these;
Where, if I were not so tall,
I should live for good and all.

The Thirsty Pigeon
An Aesop's Fable retold by J. H. Stickney

A Pigeon who was very thirsty saw a goblet of water painted on a signboard. Without stopping to see what it was, she flew to it with a loud whir, and dashing against the signboard, jarred herself terribly. Having broken her wings, she fell to the ground, and was caught by a man who said, "Your zeal should never outrun your caution."

Exercise

In your workbook, circle the capital letter that begins each sentence and the punctuation mark that ends each sentence, and underline the exclamatory sentence from this passage:

"How on earth, Badger," he said at last, "did you ever find time and strength to do all this? It's astonishing!"

Copywork

Literature

"How on earth, Badger," he said at last, "did you ever find time and strength to do all this? It's astonishing!"

Poetry—The Flowers

All the names I know from nurse:
Gardener's garters, Shepherd's purse,
Bachelor's buttons, Lady's smock,
And the Lady Hollyhock.

59. Imperative Sentences

- The Wind in the Willows, Chapter 5

A sentence is a group of words that expresses a complete thought.

Do you know what **imperator** means in Latin? An **imperator** was a Roman general. Do you know what generals do? They give commands!

An imperative sentence gives a command or makes a request. It ends with a period.

> "Hang River Bank, and supper too! I tell you, I'm going to find this place now, if I stay out all night. So cheer up, old chap, and take my arm, and we'll very soon be back there again."

The Water Rat is speaking to Mole in these sentences from *The Wind in the Willows*. The first sentence is an exclamatory sentence that shows strong feeling. The second sentence is a declarative sentence that gives information. The third sentence is an imperative sentence. What commands or requests does he give Mole?

> Cheer up.
>
> Take my arm.

You probably hear imperative sentences every day, such as:

> Please set the table.
>
> Do your lessons.
>
> Eat your dinner.
>
> Clean your room.

Can you think of more?

The Cloud
by Sara Teasdale

I am a cloud in the heaven's height,
The stars are lit for my delight,
Tireless and changeful, swift and free,
I cast my shadow on hill and sea
But why do the pines on the mountain's crest
Call to me always, "Rest, rest"?

I throw my mantle over the moon
And I blind the sun on his throne at noon,
Nothing can tame me, nothing can bind,
I am a child of the heartless wind
But oh the pines on the mountain's crest
Whispering always, "Rest, rest."

The Lion's Share
An Aesop's Fable

A long time ago, the Lion, the Fox, the Jackal, and the Wolf agreed to go hunting together, sharing with each other whatever they found.

One day the Wolf ran down a Stag and immediately called his comrades to divide the spoil.

Without being asked, the Lion placed himself at the head of the feast to do the carving, and, with a great show of fairness, began to count the guests.

"One," he said, counting on his claws, "that is myself the Lion. Two, that's the Wolf, three, is the Jackal, and the Fox makes four."

He then very carefully divided the Stag into four equal parts.

"I am King Lion," he said, when he had finished, "so of course I get the first part. This next part falls to me because I am the strongest; and this is mine because I am the bravest."

He now began to glare at the others very savagely. "If any of you have any claim to the part that is left," he growled, stretching his claws meaningly, "now is the time to speak up."

Might makes right.

Exercise

In your workbook, circle the capital letter that begins each sentence and the punctuation mark that ends each sentence, and underline the imperative sentence from this passage:

"What is it, old fellow? Whatever can be the matter? Tell us your trouble, and let me see what I can do."

Copywork

Literature

"What is it, old fellow? Whatever can be the matter? Tell us your trouble, and let me see what I can do."

Maxim

A fool and his money are soon parted.

60. Narration: The Wolf and the Crane

- **The Wind in the Willows, Chapter 6**

It's time for a narration. Your instructor will read this fable to you, and you will tell the story back to her while she writes it down for you. Then your instructor will write part of it for you to use as copywork.

The Wolf and the Crane
An Aesop's Fable

A Wolf had been feasting too greedily, and a bone had stuck crosswise in his throat. He could get it neither up nor down, and of course he could not eat a thing. Naturally that was an awful state of affairs for a greedy Wolf.

So away he hurried to the Crane. He was sure that she, with her long neck and bill, would easily be able to reach the bone and pull it out.

"I will reward you very handsomely," said the Wolf, "if you pull that bone out for me."

The Crane, as you can imagine, was very uneasy about putting her head in a Wolf's throat. But she was grasping in nature, so she did what the Wolf asked her to do.

When the Wolf felt that the bone was gone, he started to walk away.

"But what about my reward!" called the Crane anxiously.

"What!" snarled the Wolf, whirling around. "Haven't you got it? Isn't it enough that I let you take your head out of my mouth without snapping it off?"

Expect no reward for serving the wicked.

Dulce Domum
by Kenneth Grahame

Villagers all, this frosty tide,
Let your doors swing open wide,
Though wind may follow, and snow beside,
Yet draw us in by your fire to bide;
   Joy shall be yours in the morning!

Here we stand in the cold and the sleet,
Blowing fingers and stamping feet,
Come from far away you to greet—

You by the fire and we in the street—
  Bidding you joy in the morning!

For ere one half of the night was gone,
Sudden a star has led us on,
Raining bliss and benison—
Bliss tomorrow and more anon,
  Joy for every morning!

Goodman Joseph toiled through the snow—
Saw the star o'er a stable low;
Mary she might not further go—
Welcome thatch, and litter below!
  Joy was hers in the morning!

And then they heard the angels tell
"Who were the first to cry Nowell?
Animals all, as it befell,
In the stable where they did dwell!
  Joy shall be theirs in the morning!

Copywork

Narration

Instructor: Write or print part of today's narration to use as copywork.

61. Letter to/from Mr. Toad

- The Wind in the Willows, Chapter 7

Mr. Toad is in jail! One of his friends wants to write a letter to Mr. Toad while he's in jail. What do you think the Mole would say to Mr. Toad? What about the Water Rat? The Badger?

Today, you're going to pretend to be either the Mole, the Water Rat, or the Badger and write a letter to Mr. Toad. Or, you can be Mr. Toad and write a letter from jail. Here's how.

Write the date on the top right hand side of the paper.

July 22, 2008

This is the greeting. Put a comma after the greeting.

Dear Toad,

I warned you, didn't I? But you wouldn't listen.

The body of the letter is where you write all that you want to say.

Sincerely,
Ratty

This is the closing. You may choose to close with "Love," "Yours truly," or "Sincerely." Put a comma after the closing.

Sign your name!

Many a Mickle
by Walter de la Mare

A little sound —
Only a little, a little —
The breath in a reed,
A trembling fiddle;
A trumpet's ring,
The shuddering drum;
So all the glory, bravery, hush
Of music come.

A little sound —
Only a stir and a sigh
Of each green leaf
Its fluttering neighbor by;
Oak on to oak,
The wide dark forest through —
So o'er the watery wheeling world
The night winds go.

A little sound,
Only a little, a little —
The thin high drone
Of the simmering kettle,
The gathering frost,
The click of needle and thread;
Mother, the fading wall, the dream,
The drowsy bed.

The Wolf, the Kid, and the Goat
An Aesop's Fable

    Mother Goat was going to market one morning to get provisions for her household, which consisted of but one little Kid and herself.

    "Take good care of the house, my son," she said to the Kid, as she carefully latched the door. "Do not let anyone in, unless he gives you this password: 'Down with the Wolf and all his race!'"

    Strangely enough, a Wolf was lurking near and heard what the Goat had said. So, as soon as Mother Goat was out of sight, up he trotted to the door and knocked.

    "Down with the Wolf and all his race," said the Wolf softly.

    It was the right password, but when the Kid peeped through a crack in the door and saw the shadowy figure outside, he did not feel at all easy.

    "Show me a white paw," he said, "or I won't let you in."

    A white paw, of course, is a feature few Wolves can show, and so Master Wolf had to go away as hungry as he had come.

    "You can never be too sure," said the Kid, when he saw the Wolf making off to the woods.

    Two sureties are better than one.

Exercise

In your workbook, write your letter to or from Mr. Toad.

[Note to instructor: Like the letter to Neverland, this is a creative writing assignment. Many young children have difficulty with creative writing assignments. If your child feels that this assignment is stressful rather than fun, please either skip the letter or offer plenty of help.]

Copywork

Poetry—The Flowers

> Fairy places, fairy things,
> Fairy woods where the wild bee wings,
> Tiny trees for tiny dames—
> These must all be fairy names!

62. Addressing an Envelope

- The Wind in the Willows, Chapter 8

In your workbook, address the pretend envelope to send your pretend letter. Look at Wendy's envelope on the next page if you need help remembering how. Now that you know how, you can write a real letter to send!

The return address is the address of the person who is sending the letter. We write it in the top left corner.

We place the stamp in the top right corner.

Wendy Moira Angela Darling
The House Under the Ground
Neverland

Mr. and Mrs. Darling
No. 14
London

This is where we write the address of the person who will be receiving the letter.

The Blind Man and the Lame Man
An Aesop's Fable retold by J. H. Stickney

A Blind Man, being stopped in a bad piece of road, met a Lame Man, and entreated him to help him out of the difficulty into which he had fallen.

"How can I," replied the Lame Man, "since I can scarcely drag myself along? I am lame, and you look very strong."

"I am strong enough," said the other. "I could go if I could see the way."

"Oh, then we may help each other," said the Lame Man. "If you will take me on your shoulders, we will seek our fortunes together. I will be eyes for you, and you shall be feet for me."

"With all my heart," said the Blind Man. "Let us render each other our mutual services." So he took his lame companion upon his back, and they traveled on with safety and pleasure.

Exercise

In your workbook, label the adjectives ADJ and the linking verbs LV from this passage:

"You are a good, kind, clever girl," he said, "and I am indeed a proud and a stupid toad. Introduce me to your worthy aunt, if you will be so kind."

Copywork

Bible—Matthew 6:9-13, The Lord's Prayer (2 of 3)

On earth as it is in heaven.
Give us this day our daily bread.
And forgive us our debts,
as we also have forgiven our debtors.

The Brook
by Alfred Tennyson

I come from haunts of coot and hern,
I make a sudden sally,
And sparkle out among the fern,
To bicker down a valley.

By thirty hills I hurry down,
Or slip between the ridges,
By twenty thorpes, a little town,
And half a hundred bridges.

Till last by Philip's farm I flow
To join the brimming river,
For men may come and men may go
But I go on forever.

I chatter over stony ways,
In little sharps and trebles,
I bubble into eddying bays,
I babble on the pebbles.

With many a curve my banks I fret,
By many a field and fallow,
And many a fairy foreland set
With willow-weed and mallow.

I chatter, chatter as I flow
To join the brimming river,
For men may come and men may go
But I go on forever.

I wind about, and in and out,
With here a blossom sailing,
And here and there a lusty trout,
And here and there a grayling.

And here and there a foamy flake
Upon me as I travel
With many a silver water-break
Above the golden gravel.

And draw them all along, and flow
To join the brimming river,
For men may come and men may go
But I go on forever.

I steal by lawns and grassy plots,
I slide by hazel covers;
I move the sweet forget-me-nots
That grow for happy lovers.

I slip, I slide, I gloom, I glance,
Among my skimming swallows;
I make the netted sunbeam dance
Against my sandy shallows.

I murmur under moon and stars
In brambly wildernesses;
I linger by my shingly bars;
I loiter round my cresses;

And out again I curve and flow
To join the brimming river,
For men may come and men may go
But I go on forever.

The Country School by Winslow Homer

Picture Study

1. Read the title and the name of the artist. Study the picture for several minutes, then put the picture away.

2. Describe the picture.

3. Look at the picture again. Do you notice any details that you missed before? What do you like or dislike about this painting? Does it remind you of anything?

63. Review: Sentence Types; Picture Study: The Country School

- The Wind in the Willows, Chapter 9

A sentence is a group of words that expresses a complete thought.

Now you've learned about all four types of sentences. Can you remember them all? Which punctuation marks are used for each type of sentence?

A declarative sentence makes a statement and ends with a period. An interrogative sentence asks a question and ends with a question mark. An exclamatory sentence expresses sudden or strong feeling and ends with an exclamation mark. An imperative sentence gives a command or makes a request and ends with a period.

Look at this statement that the Water Rat makes in *The Wind in the Willows*.

"Yes, it's the life, the only life, to live," responded the Water Rat dreamily.

We can change this sentence to make it other types:

"Is this the life, the only life, to live?" asked the Water Rat.
"Yes, it's the life, the only life, to live!" exclaimed the Water Rat.
"Live this life," commanded the Water Rat.

Read the following sentences from *The Wind in the Willows*. Tell what type of sentence each is, and then change it to the other sentence types.

The Water Rat was restless, and he did not exactly know why.
Our time is up!
"Couldn't you stop on for just this year?"
"Come for a row, or a stroll along the hedges, or a picnic in the woods, or something."

Windy Nights
by Robert Louis Stevenson

Whenever the moon and stars are set,
    Whenever the wind is high,
All night long in the dark and wet,
    A man goes riding by.
Late in the night when the fires are out,
Why does he gallop and gallop about?

Whenever the trees are crying aloud,
    And ships are tossed at sea,
By, on the highway, low and loud,
    By at the gallop goes he.
By at the gallop he goes, and then
By he comes back at the gallop again.

Exercise

Read each sentence and determine which type it is. In your workbook, label the nouns N, the verbs V, and the linking verb LV from this passage:

"Why, where are you off to, Ratty?" asked the Mole.

"Going South, with the rest of them," murmured the Rat in a dreamy monotone. "Seawards first and then on shipboard, and so to the shores that are calling me!"

Remember, the state of being verbs can act as either linking verbs OR helping verbs.

Copywork

Literature

"Going South, with the rest of them," murmured the Rat in a dreamy monotone. "Seawards first and then on shipboard, and so to the shores that are calling me!"

64. Possessive Case

- The Wind in the Willows, Chapter 10

Sometimes, we have things that belong just to us. Ignoring the fact that the motor car belonged to someone else is why Toad is in trouble, isn't it?

When we want to show in our writing that something belongs to someone or something, we add an apostrophe and an **s** (**'s**) to the end of the noun. We call these possessive nouns because they show that a person, place, thing, or idea possesses, owns, or has something. The possessive nouns are underlined in the following sentences.

<u>Toad's</u> friends are the Water Rat, the Mole, and the Badger.

<u>Badger's</u> home is in the Wild Wood.

The motor <u>car's</u> horn went poop-poop!

Toad got a ride on a <u>woman's</u> barge.

<u>Rat's</u> life is on the river.

A pronoun is a word used in the place of a noun. Do you think we can replace possessive nouns with pronouns? We can! Some pronouns show possession. The possessive pronouns are:

First person: my, mine, our, ours

Second person: your, yours

Third person: his, her, hers, its, their, theirs

Look at the sentences below. They're the same as the ones above, but the possessive nouns are missing. Which pronouns would replace the possessive nouns from the sentences above?

_____ friends are the Water Rat, the Mole, and the Badger.

_____ home is in the Wild Wood.

_____ horn went poop-poop!

Toad got a ride on _____ barge.

_____ life is on the river.

The Gourd and the Pine
An Aesop's Fable retold by J. H. Stickney

A Gourd was once planted close beside a large and noble Pine Tree. The season was kindly, and the Gourd shot itself up in a short time, climbing by the boughs and twining about them, till it covered and overtopped the Tree itself.

The leaves were so large and the flowers and fruit so fair that the Gourd, comparing them with the slender needles of the Pine, had the assurance to think itself of greater value in the comparison.

"Why," said the Gourd, "you have been more years in growing to this stature than I have been days."

"That is true, " said the Pine, "but after many winters and summers that I have endured, the many blasting colds and parching heats, you see me the same that I was long years ago. Nothing has overcome me. But when your race is put to the proof, the first blight or frost is sure to bring down that pride of yours. In an hour you are stripped of all your glory."

Exercise

In your workbook, underline the possessive noun from this passage:

> Toad's temper, which had been simmering viciously for some time, now fairly boiled over, and he lost all control of himself.

Copywork

Literature

> Toad's temper, which had been simmering viciously for some time, now fairly boiled over, and he lost all control of himself.

Poetry—The Flowers

> Tiny woods below whose boughs
> Shady fairies weave a house;
> Tiny tree-tops, rose or thyme,
> Where the braver fairies climb!

Little White Lily
by George MacDonald

Little White Lily
Sat by a stone,
Drooping and waiting
Till the sun shone.
Little White Lily
Sunshine has fed;
Little White Lily
Is lifting her head.

Little White Lily
Said: "It is good
Little White Lily's
Clothing and food."
Little White Lily
Dressed like a bride!
Shining with whiteness,
And crowned beside!

Little White Lily
Drooping with pain,
Waiting and waiting
For the wet rain.
Little White Lily
Holdeth her cup;
Rain is fast falling
And filling it up.

Little White Lily
Said: "Good again,
When I am thirsty
To have the nice rain.
Now I am stronger,
Now I am cool;
Heat cannot burn me,
My veins are so full."

Little White Lily
Smells very sweet;
On her head sunshine,
Rain at her feet.
Thanks to the sunshine,
Thanks to the rain,
Little White Lily
Is happy again.

65. Review: Adjectives

- The Wind in the Willows, Chapter 11

An adjective is a word that modifies a noun or a pronoun.

Remember that a noun only names a person, place, thing, or idea. To modify or describe a person, place, thing, or idea, we need adjectives.

Adjectives can also answer the question, **how many**. Numbers can be adjectives, but so can words like **few** and **many**.

The adjectives have been removed from this sentence from *The Wind in the Willows*:

"They took and beat them severely with sticks, creatures, and turned them out into the night, with remarks!"

Here is the sentence with the adjectives restored:

"They took and beat them severely with sticks, <u>those</u> <u>two</u> <u>poor</u> <u>faithful</u> creatures, and turned them out into the <u>cold</u> and <u>wet</u> night, with <u>many</u> <u>insulting</u> and <u>uncalled-for</u> remarks!"

Now we know that there were **two** creatures, and they were **poor** and **faithful**. **Those** points out which creatures. We know that the night was **cold** and **wet**. We know that the remarks were **many**, **insulting**, and **uncalled-for**!

Look around the room. Can you think of some adjectives to describe something you can see? Think about its size, shape, and color. How many adjectives can you think of to describe your favorite toy or your pet? Look outside and describe the weather.

The Game
by Oliver Herford

Watching a ball on the end of a string,
Watching it swing back and to,

Oh, I do think it the pleasantest thing
Ever a Kitten can do.

First it goes this way, then it goes that,
Just like a bird on the wing.
And all of a tremble I crouch on the mat
Like a Lion, preparing to spring.

And now with a terrible deafening mew,
Like a Tiger I leap on my prey,
And just when I think I have torn it in two
It is up in the air and away.

The Blind Man and the Whelp
An Aesop's Fable retold by J. H. Stickney

A Blind Man was accustomed to distinguish different animals by touching them with his hands.

The whelp of a wolf was brought him, with the request that he should feel it and tell what it was.

Being in doubt, he said, "I do not quite know whether it is the cub of a fox or the whelp of a wolf; but this I know full well, that it would not be safe to admit it to the sheepfold."

Exercise

In your workbook, label each noun N and underline the adjectives from this passage:

> "Toad!" he said severely. "You bad, troublesome little animal! Aren't you ashamed of yourself? What do you think your father, my old friend, would have said?"

Which noun or pronoun does each adjective describe?

Copywork

Literature

> "Toad!" he said severely. "You bad, troublesome little animal! Aren't you ashamed of yourself?"

Maxim

> To be good is the mother of to do good.

66. Narration: The Hare and the Tortoise

- **The Wind in the Willows, Chapter 12**

It's time for a narration. Your instructor will read this fable to you, and you will tell the story back to her while she writes it down for you. Then your instructor will write part of it for you to use as copywork.

The Hare and the Tortoise
An Aesop's Fable

A Hare was making fun of the Tortoise one day for being so slow.

"Do you ever get anywhere?" he asked with a mocking laugh.

"Yes," replied the Tortoise, "and I get there sooner than you think. I'll run you a race and prove it."

The Hare was much amused at the idea of running a race with the Tortoise, but for the fun of the thing he agreed. So the Fox, who had consented to act as judge, marked the distance and started the runners off.

The Hare was soon far out of sight, and to make the Tortoise feel very deeply how ridiculous it was for him to try a race with a Hare, he lay down beside the course to take a nap until the Tortoise should catch up.

The Tortoise meanwhile kept going slowly but steadily, and, after a time, passed the place where the Hare was sleeping. But the Hare slept on very peacefully; and when at last he did wake up, the Tortoise was near the goal. The Hare now ran his swiftest, but he could not overtake the Tortoise in time.

The race is not always to the swift.

Foreign Lands
by Robert Louis Stevenson

Up into the cherry tree
Who should climb but little me?
I held the trunk with both my hands
And looked abroad in foreign lands.

I saw the next door garden lie,
Adorned with flowers, before my eye,

And many pleasant places more
That I had never seen before.

I saw the dimpling river pass
And be the sky's blue looking-glass;
The dusty roads go up and down
With people tramping in to town.

If I could find a higher tree
Farther and farther I should see,
To where the grown-up river slips
Into the sea among the ships,

To where the roads on either hand
Lead onward into fairy land,
Where all the children dine at five,
And all the playthings come alive.

Oral Exercise

Can you think of adjectives to describe the Hare and the Tortoise?

Copywork

Narration

Instructor: Write or print part of today's narration to use as copywork.

67. Commas in a Series

- Alice's Adventures in Wonderland, Chapter 1

Conjunctions are special words that help us to join words or groups of words together. You've learned about three conjunctions: and, but, or.

Look at this sentence:

Alice and the rabbit went down the rabbit-hole.
Alice drank from the bottle and ate the small cake.

In the first sentence, we use the conjunction **and** to join **Alice** and **rabbit** because they both went down the rabbit-hole. In the second sentence, **and** joins groups of words. **And** joins **drank from the bottle** with **ate the small cake** because Alice did both of these things.

Sometimes, we might want to join more than just two words or groups of words. Instead of using the conjunction **and** so many times, we can join more than two words or groups of words in another way. We can use commas!

The children ran and skipped and hopped and played.
The children ran, skipped, hopped, and played.

For breakfast, we had eggs and bacon and hash browns and milk.
For breakfast, we had eggs, bacon, hash browns, and milk.

Note that each word in our list except for the last one is followed by a comma instead of the conjunction **and**. We only use the conjunction **and** before the last word in our list.

Make a sentence that has a list of more than two items. You might want to choose animals that are on a farm, animals you have seen at the zoo, your favorite toys, or your favorite foods to eat. Ask your instructor to write it in your workbook, and tell your instructor where to place the commas!

How the Leaves Came Down
by Susan Coolidge

"I'll tell you how the leaves came down,"
  The great Tree to his children said:
"You're getting sleepy, Yellow and Brown,
  Yes, very sleepy, little Red.
  It is quite time to go to bed."

"Ah!" begged each silly, pouting leaf,
  "Let us a little longer stay;
Dear Father Tree, behold our grief!
  'Tis such a very pleasant day,
  We do not want to go away."

So, for just one more merry day
  To the great Tree the leaflets clung,
Frolicked and danced, and had their way,
  Upon the autumn breezes swung,
  Whispering all their sports among—

"Perhaps the great Tree will forget,
  And let us stay until the spring,
If we all beg, and coax, and fret."
  But the great Tree did no such thing;
  He smiled to hear their whispering.

"Come, children, all to bed," he cried;
  And ere the leaves could urge their prayer,
He shook his head, and far and wide,
  Fluttering and rustling everywhere,
  Down sped the leaflets through the air.

I saw them; on the ground they lay,
  Golden and red, a huddled swarm,
Waiting till one from far away,
  White bedclothes heaped upon her arm,
  Should come to wrap them safe and warm.

The great bare Tree looked down and smiled.
  "Good-night, dear little leaves," he said.
And from below each sleepy child
  Replied, "Good-night," and murmured,
  "It is so nice to go to bed!"

Jupiter and the Bee
An Aesop's Fable retold by J. H. Stickney

A Bee made Jupiter a present of a pot of honey, which was so kindly taken that he bade her ask what she would in exchange.

The Bee, who was nursing a private spite for the loss of some of her winter's store, desired of Jupiter that wherever she should set her sting it might be mortal.

Jupiter was loath to leave mankind at the mercy of a little spiteful insect, and was annoyed at the ill nature shown in her wish. He said, therefore, that while, for his promises's sake, he would give her the power to harm, she must be careful how she used the power, for where she planted her sting, she would leave it, and would thereby risk her own life.

Ill will often does greater harm to the one who acts from it than to the one on whom it falls.

Exercise

In your workbook, circle the commas and label the conjunction CJ from this passage:

> It had, in fact, a sort of mixed flavor of cherry tart, custard, pineapple, roast turkey, toffy, and hot buttered toast.

Copywork

Literature

> It had, in fact, a sort of mixed flavor of cherry tart, custard, pineapple, roast turkey, toffy, and hot buttered toast.

Poetry—The Flowers

> Fair are grown-up people's trees,
> But the fairest woods are these;
> Where, if I were not so tall,
> I should live for good and all.

68. Predicate Adjectives

- Alice's Adventures in Wonderland, Chapter 2

**An adjective is a word that
modifies a noun or a pronoun.**

Adjectives tell us the baby is **happy**, the barn is **red**, the soup is **delicious**, and the day is **hot**. Happy, red, delicious, and hot are all adjectives. They tell us more about nouns.

>   The <u>happy</u> baby is playing.
>   The baby is <u>happy</u>.

Both of these examples are ways to use adjectives to modify nouns and pronouns. In the first sentence, we tell what the happy baby is doing. In the second sentence, we use a linking verb to say that the baby is happy. The linking verb **is** connects **baby** to **happy**. In both sentences, the word **happy** is an adjective that describes the baby. In the sentences below, which adjective describes the boy?

>   The sick boy coughed and sneezed.
>   The boy is sick.

Think of a noun and an adjective to describe it. Can you make a pair of sentences about your noun? In one sentence, use a linking verb to link the noun to the adjective. In the other, tell what the noun is doing.

Where Go the Boats?
by Robert Louis Stevenson

Dark brown is the river,
    Golden is the sand.
It flows along for ever,
    With trees on either hand.

Green leaves a-floating,
    Castles of the foam,
Boats of mine a-boating—
    Where will all come home?

On goes the river
    And out past the mill,
Away down the valley,
    Away down the hill.

Away down the river,
    A hundred miles or more,
Other little children
    Shall bring my boats ashore.

Mercury and the Woodman
An Aesop's Fable retold by J. H. Stickney

A Woodman, felling a tree by the side of the river, let his ax drop by accident into the stream.

Being thus suddenly deprived of the tool by means of which he gained his livelihood, he sat down upon the bank and lamented his hard fate.

To his surprise Mercury appeared and asked him what was the matter. Having heard the story of the man's misfortune, he dived to the bottom of the river, and bringing up a golden ax, inquired if that was the one he had lost.

On saying that it was not his, Mercury dived a second time, and returning with a silver ax in his hand, again demanded of the Woodman if it was his.

This also the Woodman refused, saying that it was none of his. Mercury disappeared a third time and brought up the ax that the man had lost. This the poor man took with joy and thankfulness.

So pleased was Mercury with the honesty of the man, that he gave him the other two axes in addition to his own.

The Woodman, on his return home, related to his companions all that had happened. One of them resolved to see if he could secure the same good fortune to himself.

He ran to the river and threw his ax in, then sat down upon the bank to lament his sad fate.

Mercury appeared as before and demanded to know the cause of his grief. After hearing the man's account, he dived and brought up a golden ax and asked the man if that was his.

Transported at the sight of the precious metal, the fellow eagerly attempted to snatch it. The god, detecting his falsehood and greed, not only declined to give him the golden ax but refused to recover for him his own.

Exercise

In your workbook, label the verbs V and the linking verb LV from this passage:

> Alice took up the fan and gloves, and, as the hall was very hot, she kept fanning herself all the time she went on talking.

Which two words does the linking verb connect together?

Copywork

Literature

"Curiouser and curiouser!" cried Alice (she was so much surprised, that for the moment she quite forgot how to speak good English).

Bible—Matthew 6:9-13, The Lord's Prayer (3 of 3)

And do not lead us into temptation,
but deliver us from evil.
For Yours is the kingdom and the
power and the glory forever. Amen.

Sponge Fishing, Nassau by Winslow Homer

Picture Study

1. Read the title and the name of the artist. Study the picture for several minutes, then put the picture away.

2. Describe the picture.

3. Look at the picture again. Do you notice any details that you missed before? What do you like or dislike about this painting? Does it remind you of anything?

69. Possessive Case; Homophones; Picture Study: Sponge Fishing, Nassau

- Alice's Adventures in Wonderland, Chapter 3

Possessive nouns and pronouns show that something belongs to a person, place, thing, or idea.

The animals were wet from <u>Alice's</u> tears.

The <u>Mouse's</u> dry speech was unpopular.

The <u>race's</u> winners received prizes.

The prizes were <u>Alice's</u> comfits.

Make a sentence about something that belongs to someone. Use a possessive noun in your sentence.

Complete these sentences with a possessive pronoun:

The animals received prizes after the Caucus-race. The prizes were _____.

Alice listened to the Mouse's story. Alice listened to _____ story.

Dinah is Alice's cat. Dinah is _____ cat.

Homophones are words that have the same pronunciation but different meanings.

Homophones are words that sound the same but have different meanings. They are sometimes spelled differently, too.

My ball is <u>red</u>. I <u>read</u> this book yesterday.

I can't <u>hear</u> you! Ready or not, <u>here</u> I come!

<u>Would</u> you like to come to the party? The chair is made of <u>wood</u>.

Lewis Carroll, the author of *Alice's Adventures in Wonderland*, often used homophones to make jokes. Sometimes a person in the story will say something, and another character will think he meant something else!

Love Between Brothers and Sisters
by Isaac Watts

Whatever brawls disturb the street,
  There should be peace at home;
Where sisters dwell and brothers meet,
  Quarrels should never come.

Birds in their little nests agree;
  And 'tis a shameful sight,
When children of one family
  Fall out and chide and fight.

Exercise

In your workbook, underline the possessive nouns and pronouns and circle the homophones from this passage:

> "Mine is a long and a sad tale!" said the Mouse, turning to Alice, and sighing.
>
> "It is a long tail, certainly," said Alice, looking down with wonder at the Mouse's tail, "but why do you call it sad?"

Copywork

Literature

> "It is a long tail, certainly," said Alice, looking down with wonder at the Mouse's tail, "but why do you call it sad?"

70. The Ten Commandments

- Alice's Adventures in Wonderland, Chapter 4

You've learned about imperative sentences which give a command or make a request. In the Bible, there are Ten Commandments that God gave to Moses in Exodus 20:2-17.

The Ten Commandments

1. You shall have no other gods before Me.

2. You shall not make for yourself a carved image, or any likeness of anything that is in heaven above, or that is in the earth beneath, or that is in the water under the earth.

3. You shall not take the name of the Lord your God in vain.

4. Remember the Sabbath day, to keep it holy.

5. Honor your father and your mother, that your days may be long in the land that the Lord your God is giving you.

6. You shall not murder.

7. You shall not commit adultery.

8. You shall not steal.

9. You shall not bear false witness against your neighbor.

10. You shall not covet your neighbor's house; you shall not covet your neighbor's wife, or his male servant, or his female servant, or his ox, or his donkey, or anything that is your neighbor's.

[Instructor: I highly recommend Elton Trueblood's poem "The Ten Commandments in Verse" for memorizing the order of the Ten Commandments. It is not in the public domain, but it can be found easily on the internet.]

Hide and Seek
by Walter de la Mare

Hide and seek, says the Wind,
   In the shade of the woods;
Hide and seek, says the Moon,
   To the hazel buds;
Hide and seek, says the Cloud,
   Star on to star;
Hide and seek, says the Wave,
   At the harbour bar;
Hide and seek, say I,
   To myself, and step
Out of the dream of Wake
   Into the dream of Sleep.

The Mules and the Robbers
An Aesop's Fable retold by J. H. Stickney

Two Mules, laden with packs, were trudging along the highway. One carried panniers filled with money, the other sacks of grain.

The Mule that carried the treasure walked with head erect and stately step, jingling the bells about his neck as he went.

His companion followed at a quiet easy pace.

Suddenly a band of Robbers sprang upon them, attracted by the strong proud step and the jingling bells. The Mule that carried the gold made so great an ado that the Robbers seized his pack, wounding him with their weapons, and hearing footsteps, fled.

"I am glad," said the other, "that I was thought of so little consequence for I have lost nothing, nor am I hurt with any wound."

Exercise

In your workbook, circle the ending punctuation mark and name the sentence type of each of the sentences from this passage:

> "Don't be particular. Here, Bill! Catch hold of this rope. Will the roof bear? Mind that loose slate. Oh, it's coming down! Heads below!"

Copywork

Literature

"Don't be particular. Here, Bill! Catch hold of this rope. Will the roof bear? Mind that loose slate. Oh, it's coming down! Heads below!"

Poetry—Hide and Seek

Hide and seek, says the Wind,
    In the shade of the woods;
Hide and seek, says the Moon,
    To the hazel buds;

71. Review: Nouns, Pronouns, Adjectives, Verbs

- Alice's Adventures in Wonderland, Chapter 5

Are you ready to show how much you've learned? Start by saying the definition of a noun, a pronoun, a verb, and an adjective. Ready now?

First, think of some nouns. Can you think of three people? Three places? Three things? Three ideas? Pick the three you like best and write them (or ask your instructor to write them) on the first set of lines in your workbook.

Second, think of a pronoun that could replace each of the nouns. Write them on the second set of lines in your workbook.

Third, think of an adjective that describes each noun. Write them on the third set of lines in your workbook.

Fourth, think of an action verb that each of those nouns could do and write them on the fourth set of lines in your workbook.

Now, have some fun with them. Can you make sentences with the words you chose? Can you make silly sentences by mixing up the verbs and adjectives for your nouns?

The Captain's Daughter
by James T. Fields

We were crowded in the cabin,
   Not a soul would dare to sleep,—
It was midnight on the waters,
   And a storm was on the deep.

'Tis a fearful thing in winter
   To be shattered by the blast,
And to hear the rattling trumpet
   Thunder, "Cut away the mast!"

So we shuddered there in silence,—
   For the stoutest held his breath,
While the hungry sea was roaring
   And the breakers talked with Death.

As thus we sat in darkness,
   Each one busy with his prayers,
"We are lost!" the captain shouted
   As he staggered down the stairs.

But his little daughter whispered,
   As she took his icy hand,
"Isn't God upon the ocean,
   Just the same as on the land?"

Then we kissed the little maiden.
   And we spoke in better cheer,
And we anchored safe in harbor
   When the morn was shining clear.

The Farthing Rushlight
An Aesop's Fable retold by J. H. Stickney

A Rushlight, in love with its own brilliancy, once boasted that its light was brighter even than that of the sun, the moon, and the stars.

Just then a door opened, and a puff of wind blew it out.

As the owner relighted it, he said: "Cease now your boasting. Be content to shine in silence. Heavenly lights do not blow out. Know that not even the stars need to be relit."

Exercise

In your workbook, label the pronouns PRO from this passage:

> Alice thought she might as well wait, as she had nothing else to do, and perhaps after all it might tell her something worth hearing.

Copywork

Literature

> Alice thought she might as well wait, as she had nothing else to do, and perhaps after all it might tell her something worth hearing.

Maxim

> A good beginning makes a good ending.

72. Hercules and the Wagoner

- Alice's Adventures in Wonderland, Chapter 6

It's time for a narration. Your instructor will read this fable to you, and you will tell the story back to her while she writes it down for you. Then your instructor will write part of it for you to use as copywork.

Hercules and the Wagoner
An Aesop's Fable

    A Farmer was driving his wagon along a miry country road after a heavy rain. The horses could hardly drag the load through the deep mud, and at last came to a standstill when one of the wheels sank to the hub in a rut.

    The Farmer climbed down from his seat and stood beside the wagon looking at it but without making the least effort to get it out of the rut. All he did was to curse his bad luck and call loudly on Hercules to come to his aid. Then, it is said, Hercules really did appear, saying:

    "Put your shoulder to the wheel, man, and urge on your horses. Do you think you can move the wagon by simply looking at it and whining about it? Hercules will not help unless you make some effort to help yourself."

    And when the Farmer put his shoulder to the wheel and urged on the horses, the wagon moved very readily, and soon the Farmer was riding along in great content and with a good lesson learned.

    Self help is the best help.

    Heaven helps those who help themselves.

The Nightingale and the Glow-Worm
by William Cowper

A nightingale, that all day long
Had cheered the village with his song,
Nor yet at eve his note suspended,
Nor yet when eventide was ended,
Began to feel, as well he might,
The keen demands of appetite;
When, looking eagerly around,
He spied far off, upon the ground,

A something shining in the dark,
And knew the glow-worm by his spark;
So, stooping down from hawthorn top,
He thought to put him in his crop.
The worm, aware of his intent,
Harangued him thus, right eloquent:
"Did you admire my lamp," quoth he,
"As much as I your minstrelsy,
You would abhor to do me wrong,
As much as I to spoil your song;
For 'twas the self-same power divine,
Taught you to sing and me to shine;
That you with music, I with light,
Might beautify and cheer the night."
The songster heard his short oration,
And warbling out his approbation,
Released him, as my story tells,
And found a supper somewhere else.

Copywork

Narration

Instructor: Write or print part of today's narration to use as copywork.

73. Definition: Preposition

- Alice's Adventures in Wonderland, Chapter 7

A preposition is a word that shows the relationship between a noun or a pronoun and another word in the sentence.

Now, let's talk about what that definition means. Right now, you are probably sitting. Are you sitting **on** a chair? **On** is a preposition because it shows the relationship between you and the chair. It shows where you are in relation to the chair: **on** it! Your books are **on** the bookshelf. **On** shows the relationship between **your books** and **the bookshelf**. Your school supplies might be **on** the table. **On** shows the relationship between **your school supplies** and **the table**. Do you sometimes run **around** the yard? **Around** is another preposition. It shows the relationship between **run** and **the yard**. It tells where you run.

Soon you will begin to learn a long list of prepositions.

[Instructor: Many prepositions can also be adverbs. Don't worry in the coming lessons if the child points out an adverb as a preposition. He's not forming any bad habits, and he'll learn how to tell adverbs and prepositions apart in a later lesson. Wondering if you should memorize the list of prepositions? See the appendix, Memorizing Prepositions, Pros and Cons.]

The Elf and the Dormouse
by Oliver Herford

Under a toadstool crept a wee Elf,
Out of the rain to shelter himself.
Under the toadstool, sound asleep,
Sat a big Dormouse all in a heap.
Trembled the wee Elf, frightened, and yet
Fearing to fly away lest he get wet.
To the next shelter—maybe a mile!
Sudden the wee Elf smiled a wee smile,
Tugged till the toadstool toppled in two.

Holding it over him, gaily he flew.
Soon he was safe home, dry as could be.
Soon woke the Dormouse—"Good gracious me!
Where is my toadstool?" loud he lamented.
—And that's how umbrellas first were invented.

The Fox in the Ice
An Aesop's Fable retold by J. H. Stickney

Very early one winter morning, during a hard frost, a Fox was drinking at a hole in the ice not far from the haunts of men.

Meanwhile, whether by accident or from negligence does not matter, the end of its tail got wet and froze to the ice.

No great harm was done; the Fox could easily remedy it. It had only to give a tolerably hard pull and leave about a score of hairs behind; then it could run home quickly before any one came.

But how could it make up its mind to spoil its tail? Such a bushy tail as it was—so ample, so golden! No; better wait a little. Surely men are sleeping still. It is even possible that a thaw may set in meanwhile. In that case it will be able to withdraw its tail easily from the ice hole.

So it waits; it goes on waiting, but its tail only freezes all the more. The Fox looks round; the day is already beginning to dawn. People are stirring; voices are to be heard. Our poor Fox begins to move wildly about, now this way and now that. But still it cannot free itself from the hole.

Luckily, a Wolf comes running that way.

"Dear friend! father!" cried the Fox, "do save me; I am all but lost!"

So the Wolf stopped and set to work to rescue the Fox. Its method was a simple one—it bit the tail clean off.

So our foolish friend went home tailless, but rejoicing that its skin was still on its back.

Copywork

Literature

A Dormouse was sitting between them, fast asleep, and the other two were using it as a cushion, resting their elbows on it, and talking over its head.

Poetry—Hide and Seek

Hide and seek, says the Cloud,
    Star on to star;
Hide and seek, says the Wave,
    At the harbour bar;

74. Prepositions

- Alice's Adventures in Wonderland, Chapter 8

A preposition is a word that shows the relationship between a noun or a pronoun and another word in the sentence.

Are you ready for the list of prepositions? Some of the most common prepositions are:

aboard, about, above, across, after, against, along, among, around, at, before, behind, below, beneath, beside, between, beyond, by, down, during, except, for, from, in, inside, into, like, near, of, off, on, onto, outside, over, past, round, since, through, throughout, till, to, toward, under, underneath, until, up, upon, with, within, without.

If you're memorizing the list, learn it in small chunks. Read the first line three times every day until it's memorized, then start on line two. Keep going until it's done.

One clue for finding prepositions is to think about this phrase: anywhere a rabbit can hop. A rabbit can hop <u>aboard</u> a ship, <u>about</u> the yard, <u>above</u> the grass, <u>across</u> the deck, <u>after</u> Alice, <u>against</u> the wind, <u>along</u> the tree line, <u>among</u> other rabbits, and <u>around</u> a tree. And when he gets tired, the rabbit can stay <u>at</u> home!

Another clue for finding prepositions is to remember pre**POSITION**. Prepositions often tell the position of nouns and pronouns.

Find the prepositions in the first stanza of "The Wind" by Robert Louis Stevenson.

The Wind
by Robert Louis Stevenson

I saw you toss the kites on high
And blow the birds about the sky;
And all around I heard you pass,
Like ladies' skirts across the grass—
    O wind, a-blowing all day long,
    O wind, that sings so loud a song!

I saw the different things you did,
But always you yourself you hid.
I felt you push, I heard you call,
I could not see yourself at all—
    O wind, a-blowing all day long,
    O wind, that sings so loud a song!

O you that are so strong and cold,
O blower, are you young or old?
Are you a beast of field and tree,
Or just a stronger child than me?
    O wind, a-blowing all day long,
    O wind, that sings so loud a song!

The Wolf and the Cat
An Aesop's Fable retold by J. H. Stickney

A Wolf ran out of the forest into a village—not to pay a visit, but to save its life; for it trembled for its skin.

The huntsman and a pack of hounds were after it.

It would fain have rushed in through the first gateway, but there was this unfortunate circumstance in the way: all the gateways were closed.

The Wolf saw a Cat on a partition fence and said pleadingly: "Vaska, my friend, tell me quickly, which of the moujiks here is the kindest, so that I may hide myself from my evil foes. Listen to the cry of the dogs and the terrible sound of the horns. All that noise is actually made in chase of me."

"Go quickly and ask Stefan," said Vaska, the Cat, "he is a very kind man."

"Quite true; only I have torn the skin off one of his sheep."

"Well, then, try Demian."

"I'm afraid he's angry with me, too; I carried off one of his kids."

"Run over there, then; Trofim lives there."

"Trofim! I should be afraid of even meeting him. Ever since the spring he has been threatening me about a lamb."

"Dear me, that's bad! But perhaps Klim will protect you."

"Oh, Vaska, I have killed one of his calves!"

"What do I hear, friend? You've quarreled with all the village," said Vaska to the Wolf.

"What sort of protection can you hope for here? No, no; our peasants are not so destitute of sense as to be willing to save you to their own hurt. And, really, you have only yourself to blame. What you have sown, that you must now reap."

Exercise

In your workbook, underline the preposition from this passage:

> Next came the guests, mostly Kings and Queens, and among them Alice recognized the White Rabbit.

Copywork

Literature

Next came the guests, mostly Kings and Queens, and among them Alice recognized the White Rabbit.

Bible—John 3:16

For God so loved the world, that He gave His only begotten Son, that whoever believes in Him shall not perish, but have eternal life.

Fifteen Sunflowers in a Vase by Vincent Van Gogh

Picture Study

1. Read the title and the name of the artist. Study the picture for several minutes, then put the picture away.

2. Describe the picture.

3. Look at the picture again. Do you notice any details that you missed before? What do you like or dislike about this painting? Does it remind you of anything?

75. Definition: Interjection; Picture Study: Fifteen Sunflowers in a Vase

- Alice's Adventures in Wonderland, Chapter 9

An interjection is a word or group of words that expresses sudden or strong feeling.

Do you remember what an exclamatory sentence is? An exclamatory sentence is a sentence that expresses sudden or strong feeling. We can also express sudden or strong feeling with just a single word. When we use a word to show sudden or strong feeling, we call it an interjection.

Can you think of a word you might say if your parents suggested going out for ice-cream after dinner? Perhaps, "Hurray!" or "Yea!" What word might your mother say to you if you were getting ready for bed very slowly? "Hurry!" What word might you exclaim if your dog ran off with your favorite toy? Maybe you would yell, "Stop!" or "No!"

Can you think of other circumstances that might cause someone to use an interjection to show sudden or strong feeling? What interjection might someone use in these circumstances?

What interjection does a pirate say?

What interjection do you use when you're really impressed?

What interjection would you use if someone stepped on your toe?

The Frost
by Hannah Flagg Gould

The Frost looked forth, one still, clear night,
And whispered, "Now I shall be out of sight;
So through the valley and over the height,
   In silence I'll take my way:
I will not go on with that blustering train,

The wind and the snow, the hail and the rain,
Who make so much bustle and noise in vain,
   But I'll be as busy as they."

Then he flew to the mountain and powdered its crest;
He lit on the trees, and their boughs he dressed
In diamond beads—and over the breast
   Of the quivering lake he spread
A coat of mail, that it need not fear
The downward point of many a spear
That hung on its margin far and near,
   Where a rock could rear its head.

He went to the windows of those who slept,
And over each pane, like a fairy, crept;
Wherever he breathed, wherever he slept,
   By the light of the moon were seen
Most beautiful things—there were flowers and trees;
There were bevies of birds and swarms of bees;
There were cities with temples and towers, and these
   All pictured in silver sheen!

But he did one thing that was hardly fair;
He peeped in the cupboard, and finding there
That all had forgotten for him to prepare—
   "Now just to set them a-thinking,
I'll bite this basket of fruit," said he,
"This costly pitcher I'll burst in three,
And the glass of water they've left for me
   Shall 'tchich!' to tell them I'm drinking."

Exercise

In your workbook, underline the interjection from this passage:

> These words were followed by a very long silence, broken only by an occasional exclamation of "Hjckrrh!" from the Gryphon, and the constant heavy sobbing of the Mock Turtle.

Copywork

Literature

> These words were followed by a very long silence, broken only by an occasional exclamation of "Hjckrrh!" from the Gryphon.

76. Prepositions

- Alice's Adventures in Wonderland, Chapter 10

A preposition is a word that shows the relationship between a noun or a pronoun and another word in the sentence.

Some of the most common prepositions are:

Aboard, about, above, across, after, against, along, among, around, at, before, behind, below, beneath, beside, between, beyond, by, down, during, except, for, from, in, inside, into, like, near, of, off, on, onto, outside, over, past, round, since, through, throughout, till, to, toward, under, underneath, until, up, upon, with, within, without.

Here are the **anywhere a rabbit can hop** sentences for the second line of prepositions. A rabbit can hop <u>before</u> breakfast. A rabbit can be <u>below</u> the ground, <u>beneath</u> the ground, and <u>beyond</u> sight. A rabbit can hop <u>behind</u> his friend, <u>beside</u> his friend, <u>between</u> two friends, or <u>by</u> himself.

Below is a stanza from "The Hawthorne Children" by Eugene Field. Can you find the prepositions?

The Hawthorne Children
by Eugene Field

The Hawthorne children liked me best
Of evenings, after tea;
For then, by general request,
I spun them yarns about the west—
And all involving Me!
I represented how I'd slain
The bison on the gore-smeared plain,
And diverse tales of wonder
I'd told of how I'd fought and bled
In injun scrimmages galore,

Till Mrs. Hawthorne quoth, "No more!"
And packed her darlings off to bed
To dream of blood and thunder!

Exercise

In your workbook, underline the prepositions from this passage:

> "Come on!" cried the Gryphon, and, taking Alice by the hand, it hurried off, without waiting for the end of the song.

Copywork

Literature

> "Come on!" cried the Gryphon, and, taking Alice by the hand, it hurried off, without waiting for the end of the song.

Poetry—Hide and Seek

> Hide and seek, say I,
>   To myself, and step
> Out of the dream of Wake
>   Into the dream of Sleep.

77. Interjections

- Alice's Adventures in Wonderland, Chapter 11

An interjection is a word or group of words that expresses sudden or strong feeling.

Because they show sudden or strong feeling, interjections are usually followed by an exclamation mark. However, if the feeling is not as strong, a comma may be used to set the interjection apart from the rest of the sentence. For instance, if your brother bumps into you, you might say, "**Hey,** that hurt!" But if your brother runs into you and knocks you down, you might say, "**Hey!** That hurt!"

Look at these interjections from *Alice's Adventures in Wonderland*. Notice that most end with exclamation marks, but one is separated from the rest of the sentence with a comma. And one interjection is two words instead of only one!

"<u>Well!</u>" thought Alice to herself, "after such a fall as this, I shall think nothing of tumbling down stairs! <u>Why,</u> I wouldn't say anything about it, even if I fell off the top of the house!"

"<u>Ugh!</u>" said the Lory, with a shiver.

"<u>Hush! Hush!</u>" said the Rabbit in a low, hurried tone.

"<u>Oh, hush!</u>" the Rabbit whispered in a frightened tone.

The Owl
by Alfred Tennyson

When cats run home and light is come,
  And dew is cold upon the ground,
And the far-off stream is dumb,
  And the whirring sail goes round,
  And the whirring sail goes round;
    Alone and warming his five wits,
    The white owl in the belfry sits.

When merry milkmaids click the latch,
  And rarely smells the new-mown hay,
And the cock hath sung beneath the thatch
  Twice or thrice his roundelay,
  Twice or thrice his roundelay;
    Alone and warming his five wits,
    The white owl in the belfry sits.

The Horse and the Stag
An Aesop's Fable retold by J. H. Stickney

A Horse once had the whole range of a meadow to himself; but when a Stag came and threatened to damage the pasture, the Horse asked a Man to assist him in ridding him of the Stag. "I will," said the Man, "if you will let me put a bit in your mouth and get upon your back so as to go and find weapons." The Horse consented, and the Man accordingly mounted. But instead of being revenged on the Stag, the Horse has been from that time the slave of Man.

Revenge is dearly punished at the price of liberty.

Exercise

In your workbook, label the interjections INJ from this passage:

> "Oh, a song, please, if the Mock Turtle would be so kind," Alice replied, so eagerly that the Gryphon said, in a rather offended tone, "Hm! No accounting for tastes!"

Copywork

Literature

> "Oh, a song, please, if the Mock Turtle would be so kind," Alice replied, so eagerly that the Gryphon said, in a rather offended tone, "Hm! No accounting for tastes!"

Maxim

> Whatever is worth doing at all is worth doing well.

78. Narration: Belling the Cat

- Alice's Adventures in Wonderland, Chapter 12

It's time for a narration. Your instructor will read this fable to you, and you will tell the story back to her while she writes it down for you. Then your instructor will write part of it for you to use as copywork.

Belling the Cat
An Aesop's Fable

The mice once called a meeting to decide on a plan to free themselves of their enemy, the Cat. At least they wished to find some way of knowing when she was coming, so they might have time to run away. Indeed, something had to be done, for they lived in such constant fear of her claws that they hardly dared stir from their dens by night or day.

Many plans were discussed, but none of there was thought good enough. At last a very young Mouse got up and said:

"I have a plan that seems very simple, but I know it will be successful. All we have to do is to hang a bell about the Cat's neck. When we hear the bell ringing we will know immediately that our enemy is coming."

All the Mice were much surprised that they had not thought of such a plan before. But in the midst of the rejoicing over their good fortune, an old Mouse arose and said:

"I will say that the plan of the young Mouse is very good. But let me ask one question: Who will bell the Cat?"

It is one thing to say that something should be done, but quite a different matter to do it.

The Village Blacksmith
by Henry Wadsworth Longfellow

Under a spreading chestnut-tree
  The village smithy stands;
The smith, a mighty man is he,
  With large and sinewy hands,
And the muscles of his brawny arms
  Are strong as iron bands.

His hair is crisp, and black, and long;
  His face is like the tan;

His brow is wet with honest sweat,
  He earns whate'er he can,
And looks the whole world in the face,
  For he owes not any man.

Week in, week out, from morn till night,
  You can hear his bellows blow;
You can hear him swing his heavy sledge,
  With measured beat and slow,
Like a sexton ringing the village bell,
  When the evening sun is low.

And children coming home from school
  Look in at the open door;
They love to see the flaming forge,
  And hear the bellows roar,
And catch the burning sparks that fly
  Like chaff from a threshing-floor.

He goes on Sunday to the church,
  And sits among his boys;
He hears the parson pray and preach,
  He hears his daughter's voice
Singing in the village choir,
  And it makes his heart rejoice.

It sounds to him like her mother's voice,
  Singing in Paradise!
He needs must think of her once more,
  How in the grave she lies;
And with his hard, rough hand he wipes
  A tear out of his eyes.

Toiling,—rejoicing,—sorrowing,
  Onward through life he goes;
Each morning sees some task begin,
  Each evening sees it close;
Something attempted, something done,
  Has earned a night's repose.

Thanks, thanks to thee, my worthy friend,
  For the lesson thou hast taught!
Thus at the flaming forge of life
  Our fortunes must be wrought;
Thus on its sounding anvil shaped
  Each burning deed and thought.

Copywork

Narration

Instructor: Write or print part of today's narration to use as copywork.

79. Prepositions

- Through the Looking-Glass and What Alice Found There, Chapter 1

A preposition is a word that shows the relationship between a noun or a pronoun and another word in the sentence.

Some of the most common prepositions are:

Aboard, about, above, across, after, against, along, among, around, at, before, behind, below, beneath, beside, between, beyond, by, down, during, except, for, from, in, inside, into, like, near, of, off, on, onto, outside, over, past, round, since, through, throughout, till, to, toward, under, underneath, until, up, upon, with, within, without.

Here are the **anywhere a rabbit can hop** sentences for the third line of prepositions. A rabbit can hop down a rabbit hole, during tea-time, except on Sundays, for hours, and from his hole. A rabbit can hop in the yard, inside his warren, and like no other. He can hop near the edge of a cliff, but let's hope he doesn't hop off the cliff!

Find the prepositions in "The Fountain."

The Fountain
by James Russell Lowell

Into the sunshine,
Full of the light,
Leaping and flashing
From morn till night!
Into the moonlight,
Whiter than snow,
Waving so flower-like
When the winds blow!
Into the starlight,
Rushing in spray,
Happy at midnight,
Happy by day!

Ever in motion,
Blithesome and cheery.
Still climbing heavenward,
Never aweary;—
Glad of all weathers,
Still seeming best,
Upward or downward,
Motion thy rest;—
Full of a nature
Nothing can tame,
Changed every moment,
Ever the same;—
Ceaseless aspiring,
Ceaseless content,
Darkness or sunshine
Thy element;—
Glorious fountain!
Let my heart be
Fresh, changeful, constant,
Upward, like thee!

The Caterpillar
by Christina Rossetti

Brown and furry
Caterpillar in a hurry,
Take your walk
To the shady leaf, or stalk,
Or what not,
Which may be the chosen spot.
No toad spy you,
Hovering bird of prey pass by you;
Spin and die,
To live again a butterfly.

The Fly and the Moth
An Aesop's Fable retold by J. H. Stickney

  A Fly alighted one night upon a pot of honey, and finding it very much to his taste, began to eat it along the edges.
  Little by little, however, he had soon crept away from the edge and into the jar, until at last he found himself stuck fast. His legs and wings had become so smeared with the honey that he could not use them.
  Just then a Moth flew by, and seeing him struggling there, said: "Oh, you foolish Fly! Were you so greedy as to be caught like that? Your appetite was too much for you."
  The poor Fly had nothing to say in reply. What the Moth said was true. But by and by, when evening came, he saw the Moth flying round a lighted candle in the giddiest way, and each time a little closer to the flame, until at last he flew straight into it and was burned.

"What!" said the Fly, "are you foolish, too? You found fault with me for being too fond of honey; yet all your wisdom did not keep you from playing with fire."

It is sometimes easier to see the foolishness of others than to detect our own.

Exercise

In your workbook, underline the prepositions from this passage:

> "There, now I think you're tidy enough!" she added, as she smoothed his hair, and set him upon the table near the Queen.

Copywork

Literature

> "There, now I think you're tidy enough!" she added, as she smoothed his hair, and set him upon the table near the Queen.

Poetry—The Caterpillar

> Brown and furry
> Caterpillar in a hurry,
> Take your walk

80. Definition: Adverb

- Through the Looking-Glass and What Alice Found There, Chapter 2

An adverb is a word that modifies a verb, an adjective, or another adverb.

You've already learned about adjectives. Adjectives modify nouns and pronouns. They can tell us more about nouns and pronouns by describing them or telling us how many.

Sometimes, we want to know more about verbs, too. If someone told you that a boy ran in a race, you might want to know more. Did he run **well** or **poorly**? Did he run **quickly** or **slowly**? **Well, poorly, quickly,** and **slowly** are all adverbs. They modify the verb ran by telling us how the boy ran.

Let's look at those adverbs again. What two letters are at the end of most of those words?

well, poorly, slowly, quickly

Three of those words end in **ly**! Many adjectives can become adverbs by adding **ly** to the end of the adjective.

The boy is quick. The boy runs quickly.

In the sentences above, **quick** is an adjective that modifies the noun **boy**. **Quickly** is an adverb that modifies the verb **runs**.

Look at these sentences from *Through the Looking-Glass*. Which verb does each adverb modify?

"Is she like me?" Alice asked eagerly.

"But that's not your fault," the Rose added kindly.

Playing Robinson Crusoe
by Rudyard Kipling

Pussy can sit by the fire and sing,
  Pussy can climb a tree,
Or play with a silly old cork and string
  To 'muse herself, not me.
But I like Binkie, my dog, because
  He knows how to behave;
So, Binkie's the same as the First Friend was,
  And I am the Man in the Cave.

Pussy will play Man-Friday till
  It's time to wet her paw
And make her walk on the window-sill
  (For the footprint Crusoe saw);
Then she fluffles her tail and mews,
  And scratches and won't attend.
But Binkie will play whatever I choose,
  And he is my true First Friend.

Pussy will rub my knees with her head,
  Pretending she loves me hard;
But the very minute I go to my bed
  Pussy runs out in the yard.

And there she stays till the morning light;
  So I know it is only pretend;
But Binkie, he snores at my feet all night,
  And he is my Firstest Friend!

The Swallow and the Other Birds
An Aesop's Fable retold by J. H. Stickney

A wise Swallow, seeing a man sow seed in a field, went behind him and picked up one of the seeds to see what it was.

She found that it was flax. "When this flax has grown," she said to herself, "the man will make it into linen thread and use it to make nets for catching us Birds."

So she went to all the Birds and told them what she had discovered, begging them to come and help her eat up the flaxseed before it should sprout. "This field," she said, "is as much ours as it is his. And while one of us can do but little, all working together can quickly remove our danger."

But the Birds would not listen to her. Not one of them could she persuade to help her pick up the seeds which the farmer had sown.

By and by the flax sprang up, and the Swallow tried again to persuade the Birds to pull the young flax before it grew large. But they all made fun of her caution and let the flax keep growing.

When she saw how heedless all the Birds were, the Swallow would have nothing more to do with them, but left the woods where they lived and came among men, building her nests in barns and along the eaves of houses.

Exercise

In your workbook, underline the adverb from this passage:

> "O Tiger-lily," said Alice, addressing herself to one that was waving gracefully about in the wind, "I wish you could talk!"

Copywork

Literature

> "O Tiger-lily," said Alice, addressing herself to one that was waving gracefully about in the wind, "I wish you could talk!"

Bible—Galatians 6:9

> Let us not lose heart in doing good, for in due time we will reap if we do not grow weary.

First Steps by Vincent Van Gogh

Picture Study

1. Read the title and the name of the artist. Study the picture for several minutes, then put the picture away.

2. Describe the picture.

3. Look at the picture again. Do you notice any details that you missed before? What do you like or dislike about this painting? Does it remind you of anything?

81. Prepositions; Picture Study: First Steps

- Through the Looking-Glass and What Alice Found There, Chapter 3

A preposition is a word that shows the relationship between a noun or a pronoun and another word in the sentence.

Some of the most common prepositions are:

Aboard, about, above, across, after, against, along, among, around, at, before, behind, below, beneath, beside, between, beyond, by, down, during, except, for, from, in, inside, into, like, near, of, off, on, onto, outside, over, past, round, since, through, throughout, till, to, toward, under, underneath, until, up, upon, with, within, without.

Here are the **anywhere a rabbit can hop** sentences for the fourth line of prepositions. A rabbit can hop <u>on</u> the ground, <u>onto</u> the deck, <u>outside</u> his hole, <u>over</u> the flowers, <u>past</u> the cat, <u>round</u> the yard, and <u>since</u> he was a baby! A rabbit can hop <u>through</u> the grass, <u>throughout</u> the fields, <u>till</u> tired, <u>to</u> the beat of a different drum, and <u>toward</u> home.

Do you know what a counterpane is? It's a covering for a bed, like a comforter or bedspread. Find the prepositions in "The Land of Counterpane."

The Land of Counterpane
by Robert Louis Stevenson

When I was sick and lay a-bed,
I had two pillows at my head,
And all my toys beside me lay,
To keep me happy all the day.

And sometimes for an hour or so
I watched my leaden soldiers go,
With different uniforms and drills,
Among the bed-clothes, through the hills;

And sometimes sent my ships in fleets
All up and down among the sheets;
Or brought my trees and houses out,
And planted cities all about.

I was the giant great and still
That sits upon the pillow-hill,
And sees before him, dale and plain,
The pleasant land of counterpane.

Exercise

In your workbook, underline the prepositions from this passage:

> After this, Alice was silent for a minute or two, pondering. The Gnat amused itself meanwhile by humming round and round her head.

Copywork

Literature

> After this, Alice was silent for a minute or two, pondering. The Gnat amused itself meanwhile by humming round and round her head.

82. Adverbs

• Through the Looking-Glass and What Alice Found There, Chapter 4

An adverb is a word that modifies a verb, an adjective, or another adverb.

We've talked about how adverbs can modify verbs. Adverbs can also modify adjectives and other adverbs. First, let's look at how adverbs can modify adjectives. Look at these lines from "The Walrus and the Carpenter."

"And that was <u>scarcely</u> <u>odd</u>, because
They'd eaten every one."

The word odd is an adjective, and the word **scarcely** is an adverb that modifies **odd**. We could say that something was **very** odd or **really** odd. **Very** and **really** would also be adverbs that would modify **odd**. But in this case, it was **scarcely** odd, which tells us that it wasn't odd at all under the circumstances!

Sometimes, we aren't just happy, we're **very** happy. Sometimes, we aren't just hungry, we're **extremely** hungry.

They looked <u>so</u> <u>exactly</u> like a couple of great schoolboys, that Alice couldn't help pointing her finger at Tweedledum, and saying "First Boy!"

"Very well," the other said, <u>rather</u> <u>sadly</u>.

In the first sentence, **exactly** is an adverb modifying **looked**. It tells how they looked: **exactly** like schoolboys! But we have another adverb to modify the adverb **exactly**. They looked **so exactly** like schoolboys. In the second sentence, **sadly** is an adverb that modifies **said**, and **rather** is an adverb that modifies the adverb **sadly**.

Thoughts
by Sara Teasdale

When I can make my thoughts come forth
To walk like ladies up and down,
Each one puts on before the glass
Her most becoming hat and gown.

But oh, the shy and eager thoughts
That hide and will not get them dressed,
Why is it that they always seem
So much more lovely than the rest?

The Cat and the Martins
An Aesop's Fable retold by J. H. Stickney

A Cat, hearing that some Birds who lived in a martin box near by were ill, put on his spectacles and his overcoat, and made himself look as much as possible like a doctor, and went and knocked at their door.

"I hear that you are all sick," said he, "and have come to call on you. Let me in, and I will give you some medicine and cure you."

"No, thank you," said the Birds, who saw his whiskers and knew he was their enemy the Cat. "We are well enough — much better than if we should open our door and let you in."

Exercise

In your workbook, underline the adverbs from this passage:

> "I was thinking," Alice said very politely, "which is the best way out of this wood. It's getting so dark. Would you tell me, please?"

Copywork

Literature

> "I was thinking," Alice said very politely, "which is the best way out of this wood. It's getting so dark. Would you tell me, please?"

Poetry—The Caterpillar

> To the shady leaf, or stalk,
> Or what not,
> Which may be the chosen spot.

83. Prepositions

- Through the Looking-Glass and What Alice Found There, Chapter 5

A preposition is a word that shows the relationship between a noun or a pronoun and another word in the sentence.

Some of the most common prepositions are:

Aboard, about, above, across, after, against, along, among, around, at, before, behind, below, beneath, beside, between, beyond, by, down, during, except, for, from, in, inside, into, like, near, of, off, on, onto, outside, over, past, round, since, through, throughout, till, to, toward, under, underneath, until, up, upon, with, within, without.

Here are the anywhere a rabbit can hop sentences for the last line of prepositions. A rabbit can hop <u>toward</u> his friend, <u>under</u> the hedge, <u>underneath</u> the porch, <u>until</u> sundown, and <u>up</u> a hill. A rabbit can hop once <u>upon</u> a time, <u>with</u> friends, <u>within</u> a circle, and <u>without</u> ceasing.

Read "The Moon" by Emily Dickinson. Can you find the prepositions?

The Moon
by Emily Dickinson

The moon was but a chin of gold
A night or two ago,
And now she turns her perfect face
Upon the world below.
Her forehead is of amplest blond;
Her cheek like beryl stone;
Her eye unto the summer dew
The likest I have known.
Her lips of amber never part;
But what must be the smile
Upon her friend she could bestow
Were such her silver will!

And what a privilege to be
But the remotest star!
For certainly her way might pass
Beside your twinkling door.
Her bonnet is the firmament,
The universe her shoe,
The stars the trinkets at her belt,
Her dimities of blue.

The Cock and the Fox
An Aesop's Fable retold by J. H. Stickney

A Fox went prowling about a farmyard, not seeing a trap which the farmer had hidden there to catch him. Snap! went the trap, and the Fox found himself held fast by a strong cord. He howled horribly and was almost beside himself with rage.

A Cock, hearing the noise, flew to the top of the fence. Looking over, he saw the Fox and was terribly frightened — not daring to go near him, even when he found that his old enemy could not move. But he could not refrain from giving an exulting crow.

The Fox, looking up, said: "Dear Mr. Cock, you see how unlucky I have been, and all because I came here to inquire after your health. Do please help me to break this string, or at least do not let any one know that I am caught until I have time to gnaw it with my teeth.

The Cock said nothing, but went as fast as he could and told his master all about it. So the crafty Fox was served as the Cock thought he deserved to be.

Exercise

In your workbook, underline the prepositions from this passage:

> The boat glided gently on, sometimes among beds of weeds, and sometimes under trees, but always with the same tall riverbanks frowning over their heads.

Copywork

Literature

> The boat glided gently on, sometimes among beds of weeds, and sometimes under trees, but always with the same tall riverbanks frowning over their heads.

Maxim

> A good name is rather to be chosen than great riches.

84. Narration: The Bundle of Sticks

- Through the Looking-Glass and What Alice Found There, Chapter 6

It's time for a narration. Your instructor will read this fable to you, and you will tell the story back to her while she writes it down for you. Then your instructor will write part of it for you to use as copywork.

The Bundle of Sticks
An Aesop's Fable

A certain Father had a family of Sons, who were forever quarreling among themselves. No words he could say did the least good, so he cast about in his mind for some very striking example that should make them see that discord would lead them to misfortune.

One day when the quarreling had been much more violent than usual and each of the Sons was moping in a surly manner, he asked one of them to bring him a bundle of sticks. Then handing the bundle to each of his Sons in turn he told them to try to break it. But although each one tried his best, none was able to do so.

The Father then untied the bundle and gave the sticks to his Sons to break one by one. This they did very easily.

"My Sons," said the Father, "do you not see how certain it is that if you agree with each other and help each other, it will be impossible for your enemies to injure you? But if you are divided among yourselves, you will be no stronger than a single stick in that bundle."

In unity is strength.

The Butterfly and the Bee
by William Lisle Bowles

Methought I heard a butterfly
   Say to a laboring bee:
"Thou hast no colors of the sky
   On painted wings like me."

"Poor child of vanity! those dyes,
   And colors bright and rare,"

With mild reproof, the bee replies,
  "Are all beneath my care.

"Content I toil from morn to eve,
  And scorning idleness,
To tribes of gaudy sloth I leave
  The vanity of dress."

Copywork

Narration

Instructor: Write or print part of today's narration to use as copywork.

85. Adverbs

- Through the Looking-Glass and What Alice Found There, Chapter 7

An adverb is a word that modifies a verb, an adjective, or another adverb.

So now that we've covered adverbs that modify verbs, adjectives, and other adverbs, you know everything there is to know about adverbs, right? Not!

> They were in such a cloud of dust, that at first Alice could <u>not</u> make out which was which.

> "I could <u>not</u> send all the horses, you know, because two of them are wanted in the game."

> "I am <u>not</u> so sure of that," said the Unicorn.

In the sentences above from *Through the Looking-Glass*, the word **not** is an adverb. In the first sentence, it modifies the verb **could make**. In the second sentence, it modifies the verb **could send**. In the third sentence, **not** modifies the linking verb **am**. What adjective does the adverb **so** modify in that sentence?

Adverbs can also modify verbs to tell us about time: about when, how often, or how long an action occurs. Words like **today**, **yesterday**, **daily**, and **briefly** are all adverbs that tell us about when events occur.

> She thought that in all her life she had <u>never</u> seen soldiers so uncertain on their feet. They were <u>always</u> tripping over something or other.

In the sentences above, **never** and **always** are adverbs that tell us about time. **Never** modifies the verb **had seen**, and **always** modifies the verb **were tripping**. These adverbs tell us about how often these actions occur.

Loveliest of Trees

by A. E. Housman

Loveliest of trees, the cherry now
Is hung with bloom along the bough,
And stands about the woodland ride,
Wearing white for Eastertide.

Now, of my threescore years and ten,
Twenty will not come again,
And take from seventy springs a score,
It only leaves me fifty more.

And since to look at things in bloom
Fifty springs are little room,
About the woodlands I will go
To see the cherry hung with snow.

The Monkey and the Cat

An Aesop's Fable

Once upon a time a Cat and a Monkey lived as pets in the same house. They were great friends and were constantly in all sorts of mischief together. What they seemed to think of more than anything else was to get something to eat, and it did not matter much to them how they got it.

One day they were sitting by the fire, watching some chestnuts roasting on the hearth. How to get them was the question.

"I would gladly get them," said the cunning Monkey, "but you are much more skillful at such things than I am. Pull them out and I'll divide them between us."

Pussy stretched out her paw very carefully, pushed aside some of the cinders, and drew back her paw very quickly. Then she tried it again, this time pulling a chestnut half out of the fire. A third time and she drew out the chestnut. This performance she went through several times, each time singeing her paw severely. As fast as she pulled the chestnuts out of the fire, the Monkey ate them up.

Now the master came in, and away scampered the rascals, Mistress Cat with a burnt paw and no chestnuts. From that time on, they say, she contented herself with mice and rats and had little to do with Sir Monkey.

The flatterer seeks some benefit at your expense.

Exercise

In your workbook, label the adverbs ADV from this passage:

> Alice could not help her lips curling up into a smile as she began. "Do you know, I always thought Unicorns were fabulous monsters, too! I never saw one alive before!"

Copywork

Literature

"Do you know, I always thought Unicorns were fabulous monsters, too! I never saw one alive before!"

Poetry—The Caterpillar

No toad spy you,
Hovering bird of prey pass by you;
Spin and die,
To live again a butterfly.

86. Review: Prepositions

- Through the Looking-Glass and What Alice Found There, Chapter 8

Recite the list of prepositions, then read "Daffodils" by William Wordsworth. Can you find all of the prepositions? There are twenty-four in all.

Daffodils
by William Wordsworth

I wandered lonely as a cloud
That floats on high o'er vales and hills,
When all at once I saw a crowd,
A host, of golden daffodils;
Beside the lake, beneath the trees,
Fluttering and dancing in the breeze.
Continuous as the stars that shine
And twinkle on the milky way,
They stretched in never-ending line
Along the margin of a bay:
Ten thousand saw I at a glance,
Tossing their heads in sprightly dance.
The waves beside them danced; but they
Out-did the sparkling waves in glee:
A poet could not but be gay,
In such a jocund company:
I gazed—and gazed—but little thought
What wealth the show to me had brought:
For oft, when on my couch I lie
In vacant or in pensive mood,
They flash upon that inward eye
Which is the bliss of solitude;
And then my heart with pleasure fills,
And dances with the daffodils.

The Drum and the Vase of Sweet Herbs
An Aesop's Fable retold by J. H. Stickney

A Drum once boasted to a Vase of Sweet Herbs in this way: "Listen to me! My voice is loud and can be heard far off. I stir the hearts of men so that when they hear my bold roaring they march out bravely to battle."

The Vase spoke no words, but gave out a fine, sweet perfume, which filled the air and seemed to say: "I cannot speak, and it is not well to be proud, but I am full of good things that are hidden within me, and that gladly come forth to give cheer and comfort. People are drawn to me in their need, and they remember me afterward with gratitude. But you have nothing in you but noise, and you must be struck to make you give that out. I would not boast so much if I were you."

Exercise

In your workbook, label the prepositions PREP from this passage:

> "I always do," said the Red Knight, and they began banging away at each other with such fury that Alice got behind a tree to be out of the way of the blows.

Copywork

Literature

> "I always do," said the Red Knight, and they began banging away at each other with such fury that Alice got behind a tree to be out of the way of the blows.

Bible—1 Thessalonians 5:16-18

> Rejoice always; pray without ceasing; in everything give thanks; for this is God's will for you in Christ Jesus.

Irises by Vincent Van Gogh

Picture Study

1. Read the title and the name of the artist. Study the picture for several minutes, then put the picture away.

2. Describe the picture.

3. Look at the picture again. Do you notice any details that you missed before? What do you like or dislike about this painting? Does it remind you of anything?

87. Homophones; Picture Study: Irises

- Through the Looking-Glass and What Alice Found There, Chapter 9

Homophones are words that have the same pronunciation but different meanings.

In *Through the Looking-Glass*, Lewis Carroll continues to make jokes with homophones. In this chapter, poor Alice tries to explain how to make bread, and the White Queen misunderstands her instructions.

"How is bread made?"

"I know that!" Alice cried eagerly. "You take some <u>flour</u>—"

"Where do you pick the <u>flower</u>?" the White Queen asked. "In a garden, or in the hedges?"

"Well, it isn't picked at all," Alice explained. "It's <u>ground</u>—"

"How many acres of <u>ground</u>?" said the White Queen. "You mustn't leave out so many things."

There are two contractions which have homophones: **it's** and **they're**. These are sometimes confused with the possessive pronouns **its** and **their**. When you need to write one of these homophones, ask yourself: Can I say **it is** or **they are** instead? If so, you need to use the contraction! If not, use the pronoun. But don't forget about **there**, which points out a specific place! Let's practice those. Determine which homophone completes each of these sentences: it's, its, they're, their, there.

Alice went _____ to become a queen.

_____ a long way from one side of the board to the other.

The Red Queen, the White Queen, and Alice: _____ all queens now.

Alice stood with the other queens, _____ crowns all on _____ heads.

The leg of mutton made a bow, then returned to _____ dish.

Weather

Anonymous

Whether the weather be fine

Or whether the weather be not,

Whether the weather be cold

Or whether the weather be hot,

We'll weather the weather

Whatever the weather,

Whether we like it or not.

Exercise

In your workbook, underline the five homophones from this passage:

"Do you know why they're so fond of fishes, all about here?"

Copy the homophone sets in your workbook.

do	due	know	no
so	sew	here	hear
they're	their	there	

Copywork

Literature

"Do you know why they're so fond of fishes, all about here?"

88. Prepositions and Adverbs

- Through the Looking-Glass and What Alice Found There, Chapter 10-12

A preposition is a word that shows the relationship between a noun or a pronoun and another word in the sentence.

Prepositions show the relationship between **a noun or pronoun** and another word in the sentence. That means that prepositions always travel with a partner—a noun or pronoun. We call the preposition with the noun or pronoun, and any modifiers, a prepositional phrase. Look at these sentences from *Through the Looking-Glass*. The prepositional phrases are underlined.

"And you have been <u>along with me</u>, Kitty."

<u>On this occasion</u> the kitten only purred.

In the first sentence, **along with** shows the relationship between its partner, the pronoun **me**, and the verb **have been**. In the second sentence, the preposition **on** shows the relationship between its partner, **this occasion**, and the verb **purred**. The prepositional phrase **on this occasion** tells when the kitten purred.

Sometimes, you might see one of the prepositions that you've learned traveling without a noun or pronoun partner! This is because (Shh! This is Top Secret!) some prepositions have a secret identity. They can also be adverbs!

"Sit <u>up</u> a little more stiffly, dear!" Alice cried with a merry laugh.

In the sentence above, **up** has no partner. Instead, it's modifying the verb **sit**. That makes it an adverb!

Maker of Heaven and Earth
by Cecil Frances Alexander

All things bright and beautiful,
All creatures great and small,
All things wise and wonderful,
The Lord God made them all.

Each little flower that opens,
Each little bird that sings,
He made their glowing colors,
He made their tiny wings.

The rich man in his castle,
The poor man at his gate,
God made them, high or lowly,
And ordered their estate.

The purple-headed mountain,
The river running by,
The sunset, and the morning,
That brightens up the sky;

The cold wind in the winter,
The pleasant summer sun,
The ripe fruits in the garden,
He made them every one.

The tall trees in the greenwood,
The meadows where we play,
The rushes by the water,
We gather every day;—

He gave us eyes to see them,
And lips that we might tell,
How great is God Almighty,
Who has made all things well.

The Hare and the Hound
An Aesop's Fable retold by J. H. Stickney

 A Hound, having started a Hare which proved to be a capital runner, at length gave up the chase. His master, seeing it, said, "The little one is the best runner, eh?"

 "Ah, Master," answered the Dog, "it's all very well to laugh; but you do not see the difference between us. He was running for his life, while I was only running for my dinner."

Exercise

One of the prepositions you've memorized is undercover as an adverb in this passage:

 And she caught it up and gave it one little kiss.

Locate the adverb, but do not circle it or underline it! You'll blow its cover if you do.

Copywork

Literature

And she caught it up and gave it one little kiss.

Poetry—Maker of Heaven and Earth

All things bright and beautiful,
All creatures great and small,
All things wise and wonderful,
The Lord God made them all.

89. Review: Nouns, Adjectives, Verbs, Adverbs

- Review: Nouns, Adjectives, Verbs, Adverbs

Are you ready to show how much you've learned again? Start by saying the definition of a noun, an adjective, a verb, and an adverb. Ready now?

First, think of some nouns. Pick three and write them (or ask your instructor to write them) on the first set of lines in your workbook.

Second, think of an adjective that describes each noun and write them on the second set of lines in your workbook.

Third, think of an action verb that each of those nouns could do and write them on the third set of lines in your workbook.

Fourth, think of an adverb that could modify each of the verbs and write them on the fourth set of lines in your workbook.

Now, have some fun with them. Can you make sentences with the words you chose? Can you make silly sentences by mixing up the nouns, adjectives, verbs, and adverbs?

The Frog
by Hilaire Belloc

Be kind and tender to the Frog,
And do not call him names,
As "Slimy skin," or "Polly-wog,"
Or likewise "Ugly James,"
Or "Gap-a-grin," or "Toad-gone-wrong,"
Or "Bill Bandy-knees":
The Frog is justly sensitive
To epithets like these.

No animal will more repay
A treatment kind and fair;
At least so lonely people say
Who keep a frog (and, by the way,
They are extremely rare).

The Ax and the Trees
An Aesop's Fable retold by J. H. Stickney

Once upon a time a man came to a forest to ask the Trees if they would give him some wood to make a handle for his Ax.

The Trees thought this was very little to ask of them, and they gave him a good piece of hard wood. But as soon as the man had fitted the handle to his Ax, he went to work to chop down all the best Trees in the forest.

As they fell groaning and crashing to the ground, they said mournfully one to another, "Our kindness was misplaced. We suffer for our own foolishness."

Exercise

In your workbook, label the nouns N, adjectives ADJ, verbs V, and adverbs ADV from this passage:

> It is a very inconvenient habit of kittens (Alice had once made the remark) that, whatever you say to them, they always purr.

Copywork

Literature

> It is a very inconvenient habit of kittens (Alice had once made the remark) that, whatever you say to them, they always purr.

Maxim

> Do unto others as you would have others do unto you.

90. Narration: The Lion and the Mouse

- **Narration: The Lion and the Mouse**

It's time for a narration. Your instructor will read this fable to you, and you will tell the story back to her while she writes it down for you. Then your instructor will write part of it for you to use as copywork.

The Lion and the Mouse
An Aesop's Fable

A Lion lay asleep in the forest, his great head resting on his paws. A timid little Mouse came upon him unexpectedly, and in her fright and haste to get away, ran across the Lion's nose. Roused from his nap, the Lion laid his huge paw angrily on the tiny creature to kill her.

"Spare me!" begged the poor Mouse. "Please let me go and some day I will surely repay you."

The Lion was much amused to think that a Mouse could ever help him. But he was generous and finally let the Mouse go.

Some days later, while stalking his prey in the forest, the Lion was caught in the toils of a hunter's net. Unable to free himself, he filled the forest with his angry roaring. The Mouse knew the voice and quickly found the Lion struggling in the net. Running to one of the great ropes that bound him, she gnawed it until it parted, and soon the Lion was free.

"You laughed when I said I would repay you," said the Mouse. "Now you see that even a Mouse can help a Lion."

A kindness is never wasted.

The Sun Travels

by Robert Louis Stevenson

The sun is not a-bed, when I
At night upon my pillow lie;
Still round the earth his way he takes,
And morning after morning makes.

While here at home, in shining day,
We round the sunny garden play,
Each little Indian sleepy-head
Is being kissed and put to bed.

And when at eve I rise from tea,
Day dawns beyond the Atlantic Sea;
And all the children in the west
Are getting up and being dressed.

Copywork

Narration

Instructor: Write or print part of today's narration to use as copywork.

91. Review: Sentence Types

- This Week: A Wonder-Book for Girls and Boys: The Gorgon's Head

Can you list the four types of sentences and tell about each type? What type of punctuation mark ends each type of sentence?

Did you remember them all? A declarative sentence makes a statement and ends with a period. An interrogative sentence asks a question and ends with a question mark. An exclamatory sentence expresses sudden or strong feeling and ends with an exclamation mark. An imperative sentence gives a command or makes a request and ends with a period.

What sentence type is the following sentence?

"And can I assist your Majesty in obtaining it?"

It's a question! Change the sentence to the other sentence types. Here are some possible ways to do this to read after you've tried yourself:

"I can assist your Majesty in obtaining it."

"I, Perseus, can assist your Majesty in obtaining it!"

"Majesty, allow me to assist in obtaining it."

Read the following sentences and determine which type of sentence each is. Can you change each sentence to the other sentence types?

"Medusa's snakes will sting him soundly!"

"Perseus, why are you sad?"

"Well, tell me all about it, and possibly I may be of service to you."

"I am not so very sad."

The Months
by Christina Rossetti

January cold desolate;
February all dripping wet;
March wind ranges;
April changes;
Birds sing in tune
To flowers of May,
And sunny June
Brings longest day;
In scorched July
The storm-clouds fly
Lightning-torn;
August bears corn,
September fruit;
In rough October
Earth must disrobe her;
Stars fall and shoot
In keen November;
And night is long
And cold is strong
In bleak December.

The Eagle and the Fox
An Aesop's Fable retold by J. H. Stickney

One day a mother Eagle came flying out of her nest to look for food for her babies. She circled round and round, far up in the air, looking down upon the earth with her keen eyes.

By and by she saw a little baby Fox, whose mother had left it alone while, like the Eagle, she went for food.

Down came the bird, whir went her wings, and away she soared again, with the little Fox clutched fast in her claws.

The poor mother Fox just at that moment came running home to her child, and saw it being carried away.

"O Eagle!" she cried, "leave me my one little baby. Remember your own children, and how you would feel if one of them should be taken away. Oh, bring back my poor cub!"

But the cruel Eagle, thinking that the Fox could never reach her in her nest high in the pine tree, flew away with the little Fox, and left the poor mother to cry.

But the mother Fox did not stop to cry long. She ran to a fire that was burning in the field, caught up a blazing stick of wood, and ran with it in her mouth to the pine tree where the Eagle had her nest.

The Eagle saw her coming, and knew that the Fox would soon have the tree on fire, and that all her young ones would be burned. So, to save her own brood, she begged the Fox to stop, and brought her back her little one, safe and sound.

Oral Exercise

Determine which type of sentence this is:

> They had each of them a hundred enormous snakes growing on their heads, all alive, twisting, wriggling, curling, and thrusting out their venomous tongues!

Can you change the sentence to the other sentence types?

Copywork

Literature

> They had each of them a hundred enormous snakes growing on their heads, all alive, twisting, wriggling, curling, and thrusting out their venomous tongues!

Poetry—Maker of Heaven and Earth

> Each little flower that opens,
> Each little bird that sings,
> He made their glowing colors,
> He made their tiny wings.

92. Definition: Antonyms

- This Week: A Wonder-Book for Girls and Boys: The Gorgon's Head

Antonyms are words that have opposite meanings.

Did you know that there is a special name for words that are opposites? Young and old, hot and cold, soft and hard. These words are all antonyms!

Look at the words below and find an antonym for each:

   Short, skinny, high, shallow, love, smile, ugly, small.

Can you think of some other antonyms? Look around the room. Can you think of an antonym for anything you can see?

Read "Up and Down" by Walter de la Mare and find the antonyms.

Up and Down
by Walter de la Mare

Down the Hill of Ludgate,
   Up the Hill of Fleet,
To and fro and East and West
   With people flows the street;
Even the King of England
   On Temple Bar must beat
For leave to ride to Ludgate
   Down the Hill of Fleet.

The Three Tradesmen
An Aesop's Fable retold by J. H. Stickney

   A great city was once besieged, and all its inhabitants were gathered together to consider by what means it might be protected from the enemy.

A Bricklayer earnestly recommended bricks as the best materials for successful defense.

A Carpenter with equal energy proposed timber as a preferable means of defense.

Hearing which, a Currier stood up and said, "Sirs, I differ with you wholly. There is no material for resistance equal to covering of hides, and nothing in the present case so good as leather."

Every man for his own trade.

Exercise

Name an antonym for each of the underlined words from this passage:

> Perseus left the palace, but was scarcely out of hearing before Polydectes burst into a laugh, being greatly amused, wicked king
> that he was.

In your workbook, label the verbs V, linking verbs LV, adverbs ADV, and conjunctions CJ.

Copywork

Literature

> Perseus left the palace, but was scarcely out of hearing before Polydectes burst into a laugh, being greatly amused, wicked king
> that he was.

Bible—Hebrews 13:5

> Make sure that your character is free from the love of money, being content with what you have; for He Himself has said, "I will never desert you, nor will I ever forsake you."

The Starry Night by Vincent Van Gogh

Picture Study

1. Read the title and the name of the artist. Study the picture for several minutes, then put the picture away.

2. Describe the picture.

3. Look at the picture again. Do you notice any details that you missed before? What do you like or dislike about this painting? Does it remind you of anything?

93. A Poem, a Fable, and Copywork; Picture Study: The Starry Night

- This Week: A Wonder-Book for Girls and Boys: The Gorgon's Head

An Incident of the French Camp
by Robert Browning

You know, we French storm'd Ratisbon:
   A mile or so away
On a little mound, Napoleon
   Stood on our storming-day;
With neck out-thrust, you fancy how,
   Legs wide, arms lock'd behind,
As if to balance the prone brow
   Oppressive with its mind.

Just as perhaps he mus'd, "My plans
   That soar, to earth may fall,
Let once my army leader Lannes
   Waver at yonder wall,"—
Out 'twixt the battery smokes there flew
   A rider, bound on bound
Full-galloping; nor bridle drew
   Until he reach'd the mound.

Then off there flung in smiling joy,
   And held himself erect
By just his horse's mane, a boy:
   You hardly could suspect—
(So tight he kept his lips compress'd,
   Scarce any blood came through)
You look'd twice ere you saw his breast
   Was all but shot in two.

"Well," cried he, "Emperor, by God's grace
   We've got you Ratisbon!
The Marshal's in the market-place,

    And you'll be there anon
To see your flag-bird flap his vans
    Where I, to heart's desire,
Perched him!" The chief's eye flashed; his plans
    Soared up again like fire.

The chief's eye flashed; but presently
    Softened itself, as sheathes
A film the mother-eagle's eye
    When her bruised eaglet breathes;
"You're wounded!" "Nay," the soldier's pride
    Touched to the quick, he said:
"I'm killed, Sire!" And his chief beside,
    Smiling the boy fell dead.

The Partridge and the Fowler
An Aesop's Fable retold by J. H. Stickney

    A Fowler caught a Partridge, and was just going to kill it.
    "Wait a moment," said the Partridge, "don't kill me."
    "Why not?" said the Fowler.
    "Because I like to live," said the Partridge, "and, besides, if you let me go, I will bring some of my friends and neighbors here, and you can catch them, and that will be better than only one poor bird."
    "You are willing, then, that you friends and neighbors should die, to save your own life?" said the Fowler. "Wicked Partridge! You have lived long enough." And he killed it.

Exercise

In your workbook, label the nouns N, pronouns PRO, and prepositions PREP from this passage:

    "Behold it, then!" cried Perseus, in a voice like the blast of a trumpet.

Copywork

Literature

    "Behold it, then!" cried Perseus, in a voice like the blast of a trumpet.

94. Articles

- This Week: A Wonder-Book for Girls and Boys: The Golden Touch

The articles are a, an, the.

The articles—**a, an, the**—are three little words that you use so often with nouns, you probably don't even notice that you're saying them! Articles are adjectives because we use them to modify nouns. They don't describe nouns. Instead, they point out nouns.

The is a definite article because it is used to point out a specific noun. **A** and **an** are indefinite articles because they are used to point out any noun, not a specific noun. If your mother says, "Set **the** table, please," you know that she means a specific table: the dining table! If she ever says, "Set **a** table, please," you can set the coffee table instead!

Do you know why we have two indefinite articles? We use the article **an** before words that begin with vowels, and we use the article **a** before words that begin with consonants. Can you list the vowels?

The vowels are **a, e, i, o, u**. All other letters are consonants. So, to use an indefinite article with the word **apple**, we would say **an apple**.

Let's practice that. Answer the following questions with a noun, and use either **a** or **an** to modify the noun.

What type of citrus fruit is yellow and sour?

What is your favorite type of toy?

Where is your favorite place to go?

What sea creature has eight arms?

Trees
by Walter de la Mare

Of all the trees in England,
   Her sweet three corners in,
Only the Ash, the bonnie Ash
   Burns fierce while it is green.

Of all the trees in England,
   From sea to sea again,
The Willow loveliest stoops her boughs
   Beneath the driving rain.

Of all the trees in England,
   Past frankincense and myrrh,
There's none for smell, of bloom and smoke,
   Like Lime and Juniper.

Of all the trees in England,
   Oak, Elder, Elm and Thorn,
The Yew alone burns lamps of peace
   For them that lie forlorn.

The Mouse, the Frog, and the Hawk
An Aesop's Fable retold by J. H. Stickney

A Mouse, who had always lived on the land, and a Frog, who passed most of his time in the water, became friends.

The Mouse showed the Frog his nest and everything he could think of that was pleasant to see; and the Frog invited the Mouse to go home with him and see all the beautiful things that are under the water.

"Can you swim?" asked the Frog.

"Not much," said the Mouse.

"No matter," said the Frog, "I will tie your foot to my foot with a piece of this strong grass, and then I can pull you along nicely." The Frog laughed as he said this. He thought it would be good fun for him, but he well knew that the Mouse would not enjoy it.

When the Frog had tied the Mouse's foot to his own, they started together across the meadow. They soon came to the edge of the water, and the Frog jumped in, pulling the Mouse in with him.

"Oh, how cool and nice the water is, after the dry, hot land!" said the Frog, as he swam gaily about. But the poor Mouse was frightened.

"Please let me go," said he, "or I shall die."

"Oh, never mind," said the unkind Frog. "You will get used to the water. I just love it."

But soon the poor Mouse was drowned, and floated up to the top of the water, while the Frog frisked about down below.

Just then a Hawk saw the Mouse, and pounced upon it.

As he flew away with it the Frog was dragged out of the water, too, for he was still tied to the Mouse.

"Stop, stop!" cried the Frog. "Let me go. It is the Mouse you want."

"Come along," said the Hawk, "I want you both. I will eat you first, for I like Frog meat ever better then I do Mouse."

In a few moments the Hawk had made a good supper, and there was nothing left of either the false Frog or the foolish Mouse.

Exercise

In your workbook, underline the articles from this passage:

> The stranger's smile grew so very broad that it seemed to fill the room like an outburst of the sun, gleaming into a shadowy dell.

Label the adjectives ADJ and adverbs ADV.

Copywork

Literature

> The stranger's smile grew so very broad that it seemed to fill the room like an outburst of the sun, gleaming into a shadowy dell.

Poetry—Maker of Heaven and Earth

> The rich man in his castle,
> The poor man at his gate,
> God made them, high or lowly,
> And ordered their estate.

95. Antonyms

- This Week: A Wonder-Book for Girls and Boys: The Golden Touch

Antonyms are words that have opposite meanings.

Read the poem below. Then, look at the underlined words and think of an antonym for each.

Fairy and Child
by Eugene Field

Oh, listen, <u>little</u> Dear-My-Soul,
To the fairy voices calling,
For the moon is <u>high</u> in the misty sky
And the honey dew is <u>falling</u>;
To the <u>midnight</u> feast in the clover bloom
The bluebells are a-ringing,
And it's "Come away to the land of fay"
That the katydid is singing.

Oh, <u>slumber</u>, little Dear-My-Soul,
And hand in hand we'll wander
Hand in hand to the beautiful land
Of Balow, away off yonder;
Or we'll sail along in a lily leaf
Into the <u>white</u> moon's halo
<u>Over</u> a stream of mist and dream
Into the land of Balow.

Or, you shall have two <u>beautiful</u> wings
Two gossamer wings and airy,

And all the while shall the <u>old</u> moon <u>smile</u>
And think you a little fairy;

And you shall dance in the velvet <u>sky</u>,
And the silvery stars shall twinkle
And dream <u>sweet</u> dreams as over their beams
Your footfalls softly tinkle.

The Woman and Her Hen
An Aesop's Fable retold by J. H. Stickney

A Woman had a Hen that laid an egg every day. The eggs were large, and sold for a good price. The Woman often thought, as she took them to market: "How glad they all are to get my eggs! I could sell as many more just as easily."

It began to look a small thing to her to get but a single egg each day. "If I were to give a double allowance of barley, the Hen might be made to lay two eggs a day instead of one," she said.

So she doubled the food, and the Hen grew very fat and sleek; but she stopped laying eggs.

Exercise

In your workbook, label the adjectives ADJ and the adverbs ADV from this passage:

> If he loved anything better, or half so well, it was the one little maiden who played so merrily around her father's footstool.

Underline the possessive noun and the possessive pronoun in the passage.

Copywork

Literature

> If he loved anything better, or half so well, it was the one little maiden who played so merrily around her father's footstool.

Maxim

> We can do more good by being good than in any other way.

96. Narration: The Shepherd Boy and the Wolf

- **This Week:** A Wonder-Book for Girls and Boys: The Golden Touch

It's time for a narration. Your instructor will read this fable to you, and you will tell the story back to her while she writes it down for you. Then your instructor will write part of it for you to use as copywork.

The Shepherd Boy and the Wolf
An Aesop's Fable

A Shepherd Boy tended his master's Sheep near a dark forest not far from the village. Soon he found life in the pasture very dull. All he could do to amuse himself was to talk to his dog or play on his shepherd's pipe.

One day as he sat watching the Sheep and the quiet forest, and thinking what he would do should he see a Wolf, he thought of a plan to amuse himself.

His Master had told him to call for help should a Wolf attack the flock, and the Villagers would drive it away. So now, though he had not seen anything that even looked like a Wolf, he ran toward the village shouting at the top of his voice, "Wolf! Wolf!"

As he expected, the Villagers who heard the cry dropped their work and ran in great excitement to the pasture. But when they got there they found the Boy doubled up with laughter at the trick he had played on them.

A few days later the Shepherd Boy again shouted, "Wolf! Wolf!" Again the Villagers ran to help him, only to be laughed at again. Then one evening as the sun was setting behind the forest and the shadows were creeping out over the pasture, a Wolf really did spring from the underbrush and fall upon the Sheep.

In terror the Boy ran toward the village shouting "Wolf! Wolf!" But though the Villagers heard the cry, they did not run to help him as they had before. "He cannot fool us again," they said.

The Wolf killed a great many of the Boy's sheep and then slipped away into the forest.

Liars are not believed even when they speak the truth.

The Boy Who Never Told a Lie
Anonymous

Once there was a little boy,
   With curly hair and pleasant eye—
A boy who always told the truth,
   And never, never told a lie.

And when he trotted off to school,
   The children all about would cry,
"There goes the curly-headed boy—
   The boy that never tells a lie."

And everybody loved him so,
   Because he always told the truth,
That every day, as he grew up,
   'Twas said, "There goes the honest youth."

And when the people that stood near
   Would turn to ask the reason why,
The answer would be always this:
   "Because he never tells a lie."

Copywork

Narration

   Instructor: Write or print part of today's narration to use as copywork.

97. Review: Nouns, Adjectives, Verbs, Adverbs

- **This Week: A Wonder-Book for Girls and Boys: The Paradise of Children**

Are you ready to show how much you've learned again? Start by saying the definition of a noun, an adjective, a verb, and an adverb. Ready now?

First, think of some nouns. Pick three and write them (or ask your instructor to write them) on the first set of lines in your workbook.

Second, think of an adjective that describes each noun and write them on the second set of lines in your workbook.

Third, think of an action verb that each of those nouns could do and write them on the third set of lines in your workbook.

Fourth, think of an adverb that could modify each of the verbs and write them on the fourth set of lines in your workbook.

Now, have some fun with them. Can you make sentences with the words you chose? Can you make silly sentences by mixing up the nouns, adjectives, verbs, and adverbs?

Trees
by Sara Coleridge

The Oak is called the king of trees,
The Aspen quivers in the breeze,
The Poplar grows up straight and tall,
The Peach tree spreads along the wall,
The Sycamore gives pleasant shade,
The Willow droops in watery glade,
The Fir tree useful timber gives,
The Beech amid the forest lives.

The Hawk and the Nightingale
An Aesop's Fable retold by J. H. Stickney

A Nightingale sitting on the top of an oak, singing her evening song, was spied by a hungry Hawk, who swooped down and seized her. The frightened Nightingale prayed the Hawk to let her go.

"If you are hungry," said she, "why not catch some large bird? I am not big enough for even a luncheon."

"Do you happen to see many large birds flying about?" said the Hawk.

"You are the only bird I have seen to-day, and I should be foolish indeed to let you go for the sake of larger birds that are not in sight. A morsel is better than nothing."

Exercise

In your workbook, label the verbs V, linking verbs LV, and the adverbs ADV from this passage:

"How provoking!" exclaimed Pandora, pouting her lip. "I wish the great ugly box were out of the way!"

Copywork

Literature

"How provoking!" exclaimed Pandora, pouting her lip. "I wish the great ugly box were out of the way!"

Poetry—Maker of Heaven and Earth

The purple-headed mountain,
The river running by,
The sunset, and the morning,
That brighten up the sky;

98. Review: Interjections

- **This Week: A Wonder-Book for Girls and Boys: The Paradise of Children**

An interjection is a word or group of words that expresses sudden or strong feeling.

An interjection can be only one word or it can be a group of words, but it will always express sudden or strong feeling. Remember that an interjection often ends with an exclamation mark, but it can also be separated from the rest of the sentence with a comma.

Can you think of something that would cause you to use an interjection? What interjection might you use if...

...someone threw a surprise party for you?

...you dropped your favorite book in a puddle?

...you won a prize in a contest?

...a UFO landed in your front yard?

Look at these interjections from "The Paradise of Children." Notice the punctuation. Some of the interjections end with an exclamation mark while others are separated from the rest of the sentence with a comma.

"<u>Oh</u>, the most curious staff you ever saw!" cried Epimetheus.

<u>Ah</u>, naughty Pandora!

"<u>Well</u>!—<u>yes</u>!—I am resolved to take just one peep!"

"<u>Oh</u>, I am stung!" cried he.

A Pin Has a Head
by Christina Rossetti

A pin has a head, but has no hair;
A clock has a face, but no mouth there;
Needles have eyes, but they cannot see;
A fly has a trunk without lock or key;
A timepiece may lose, but cannot win;
A corn-field dimples without a chin;
A hill has no leg, but has a foot;
A wine-glass a stem, but not a root;
A watch has hands, but no thumb or finger;
A boot has a tongue, but is no singer;
Rivers run, though they have no feet;
A saw has teeth, but it does not eat;
Ash-trees have keys, yet never a lock;
And baby crows, without being a cock.

The Jackdaw and the Sheep
An Aesop's Fable retold by J. H. Stickney

A Jackdaw sat chattering upon the back of a Sheep.

"Peace, I pray you, noisy bird," said the Sheep. "You are wearing my life out. If I were a dog, you would not think of serving me so."

"That is true," replied the Jackdaw. "You are right. I never meddle with the surly and revengeful; but I love to plague gentle, helpless creatures like you, that can not do me any harm in return."

"I wonder if all cowards are not like the Jackdaw," mused the Sheep, as it went on contentedly browsing on the hillside.

Exercise

In your workbook, label the interjections INJ from this passage:

> If you were left alone with the box, might you not feel a little tempted to lift the lid? But you would not do it. Oh, fie! No, no!

Copywork

Literature

> If you were left alone with the box, might you not feel a little tempted to lift the lid? But you would not do it. Oh, fie! No, no!

Bible—Matthew 22:37

> And He said to him, "You shall love the Lord your God with all your heart, and with all your soul, and with all your mind."

Van Gogh's Room at Arles by Vincent Van Gogh

Picture Study

1. Read the title and the name of the artist. Study the picture for several minutes, then put the picture away.

2. Describe the picture.

3. Look at the picture again. Do you notice any details that you missed before? What do you like or dislike about this painting? Does it remind you of anything?

99. Review: Conjunctions; Picture Study: Van Gogh's Room at Arles

- This Week: A Wonder-Book for Girls and Boys: The Paradise of Children

A conjunction is a word that joins words or groups of words together.

So far, you've learned three conjunctions: and, but, or. Conjunctions join words or groups of words together. Which words or groups of words are joined together in these sentences?

The boys laughed <u>and</u> played. The girls laughed <u>and</u> played.
The boys <u>and</u> girls laughed <u>and</u> played.

Do you want eggs for breakfast? Do you want cereal for breakfast?
Do you want eggs <u>or</u> cereal for breakfast?

He plays the violin. She plays the piano.
He plays the violin, <u>but</u> she plays the piano.

Fill in the missing conjunctions (and, but, or) from these sentences from "The Paradise of Children":

"That is a secret, _____ you must be kind enough not to ask any questions about it."

"Most probably, it contains pretty dresses for me to wear, _____ toys for you _____ me to play with."

"Let us run out of doors, _____ have some nice play with the other children."

This was at first only the faint shadow of a Trouble; _____, every day, it grew more and more substantial.

275

A Dream
by William Blake

Once a dream did weave a shade
O'er my angel-guarded bed,
That an emmet lost its way
Where on grass methought I lay.

Troubled, wildered, and forlorn,
Dark, benighted, travel-worn,
Over many a tangled spray,
All heart-broke, I heard her say:

'O my children! do they cry,
Do they hear their father sigh?
Now they look abroad to see,
Now return and weep for me.'

Pitying, I dropped a tear:
But I saw a glow-worm near,
Who replied, 'What wailing wight
Calls the watchman of the night?'

'I am set to light the ground,
While the beetle goes his round:
Follow now the beetle's hum;
Little wanderer, hie thee home!'

Exercise

In your workbook, label the conjunctions CJ and the prepositions PREP from this passage:

> Here and there, peeping forth from behind the carved foliage, Pandora once or twice fancied that she saw a face not so lovely.

Which words or groups of words are being joined by the conjunctions?

Copywork

Literature

> Here and there, peeping forth from behind the carved foliage, Pandora once or twice fancied that she saw a face not so lovely.

100. Review: Contractions, Homophones

- **This Week: A Wonder-Book for Girls and Boys: The Three Golden Apples**

Do you remember what it's called when we take two words and make one smaller word? It's called a contraction. We use an apostrophe to show where the missing letters would be.

I am	I'm	I will	I'll
is not	isn't	are not	aren't

There are other words—homophones—that sound the same as some contractions but are spelled differently. When you write, how do you know which word to use? The easiest way is to say both words that make up the contraction. Does the sentence make sense? If it does, then use the contraction. If it doesn't, then use the other word.

Decide whether you should use **its** or **it's** in the following sentences from "The Three Golden Apples":

_____ said that there was a dragon beneath the tree, with a hundred terrible heads, fifty of which were always on the watch, while the other fifty slept.

"For, as fast as I cut off a head, two others grew in _____ place."

"But _____ my destiny to obey him."

Decide whether you should use **there's** or **theirs** in the following sentences from "The Three Golden Apples":

But _____ not, I suppose, a graft of that wonderful fruit on a single tree in the wide world.

"_____ nobody but myself," quoth the giant.

Silver
by Walter de la Mare

Slowly, silently, now the moon
Walks the night in her silver shoon:
This way, and that, she peers and sees
Silver fruit upon silver trees;
One by one the casements catch
Her beams beneath the silvery thatch;
Couched in his kennel, like a log,
With paws of silver sleeps the dog
From their shadowy cote the white breasts peep
Of doves in a silver-feathered sleep;
A harvest mouse goes scampering by,
With silver claws and silver eye;
And moveless fish in the water gleam
By silver reeds in a silver stream.

The Mouse, the Cat, and the Cock
An Aesop's Fable retold by J. H. Stickney

A young Mouse, that had not seen much of the world, came home one day and said: "O mother! I have had such a fright! I saw a great creature strutting about on two legs. I wonder what it was! On his head was a red cap. His eyes were fierce and stared at me, and he had a sharp mouth.

"All at once he stretched his long neck, and opened his mouth so wide, and roared so loud, that I thought he was going to eat me up, and I ran home as fast as I could. I was sorry that I met him, for I had just seen a lovely animal, greater even then he, and would have made friends with her. She had soft fur like ours, only it was gray and white. Her eyes were mild and sleepy, and she looked at me very gently and waved her long tail from side to side. I thought she wished to speak to me, and I would have gone near her, but that dreadful thing began to roar, and I ran away."

"My dear child," said the mother, "you did well to run away. The fierce thing you speak of would have done you no harm. It was a harmless Cock. But that soft, pretty thing was the Cat, and she would have eaten you up in a minute, for she is the worst enemy you have in the whole world. Appearances are not always to be trusted."

Exercise

In your workbook, underline the contractions and label the nouns N from this passage:

"That's no more than fair, and I'll do it!" quoth the giant. "For just five minutes, then, I'll take back the sky."

Copywork

Literature

"That's no more than fair, and I'll do it!" quoth the giant. "For just five minutes, then, I'll take back the sky."

Contractions (Optional)

    is not   are not   was not
    he is   she is   it is
    had not   could not   will not
    he will   she will   they will

Poetry—Maker of Heaven and Earth

The cold wind in the winter,
The pleasant summer sun,
The ripe fruits in the garden,
He made them every one.

101. Definition: Synonyms

- This Week: A Wonder-Book for Girls and Boys: The Three Golden Apples

Synonyms are words that have the same meaning.

Do you remember learning about antonyms? Antonyms are words that have the opposite meaning. Today we're going to learn about synonyms. Synonyms are the opposite of antonyms! They are words that have the same meaning, like small and tiny, or pretty and beautiful.

Read "Good and Bad Children" by Robert Louis Stevenson. Can you think of a synonym for each of the underlined words?

Good and Bad Children
by Robert Louis Stevenson

Children, you are very <u>little</u>,
And your bones are very brittle;
If you would grow <u>great</u> and stately,
You must try to walk <u>sedately</u>.

You must still be bright and <u>quiet</u>,
And <u>content</u> with simple diet;
And remain, through all bewild'ring,
Innocent and <u>honest</u> children.

Happy hearts and <u>happy</u> faces,
Happy play in grassy places—
That was how in <u>ancient</u> ages,
Children grew to kings and sages.

But the <u>unkind</u> and the unruly,
And the sort who eat unduly,

They must never hope for glory—
Theirs is quite a different story!

<u>Cruel</u> children, <u>crying</u> babies,
All grow up as geese and gabies,
Hated, as their age increases,
By their nephews and their nieces.

Stone Broth

An Aesop's Fable retold by J. H. Stickney

One very stormy day a Poor Man came to a rich man's house to beg.

"Away with you!" said the servants. "Do not come here troubling us."

Then said the Man, "Only let me come in and dry my clothes at your fire." This, the servants thought, would not cost them anything, so they let him come in.

The Poor Man then asked the cook to let him have a pan, so that he could make some stone broth.

"Stone broth!" said the cook. "I should like to see how you can make broth out of a stone." So she gave him a pan. The Man filled it with water from the pump, and then put into it a stone from the road. "But you must have some salt," said the cook.

"Do you think so?" courteously replied the stranger. She gave him the salt, and before long she added some peas, some mint, and thyme. At last she brought him all the scraps of meat she could find, so that the Poor Man's broth made him a good dinner.

"You see," said the Man, "that if you only try long enough, and are cheerful, making the best of what you have, you may at last get what you want."

Exercise

In your workbook, labels the nouns N, pronouns PRO, and adjectives ADJ from this passage:

O my sweet little people, you have no idea what a weight there was in that same blue sky, which looks so soft and aerial above our heads!

Remember that articles are adjectives!

Copywork

Literature

O my sweet little people, you have no idea what a weight there was in that same blue sky, which looks so soft and aerial above our heads!

Maxim

Write it on your heart that every day is the best day of the year.

102. Narration: The Arab and His Camel

- This Week: A Wonder-Book for Girls and Boys: The Three Golden Apples

It's time for a narration. Your instructor will read this fable to you, and you will tell the story back to her while she writes it down for you. Then your instructor will write part of it for you to use as copywork.

The Arab and His Camel
An Aesop's Fable retold by J. H. Stickney

As an Arab sat in his tent one cold night, he saw the curtain gently lifted, and the face of his Camel looking in.

"What is it?" he asked kindly.

"It is cold, master," said the Camel. "Suffer me, I pray thee, to hold my head within the tent."

"By all means," replied the hospitable Arab, and the Camel stood with his head inside the tent.

"Might I also warm my neck a little?" he entreated after a moment.

The Arab readily consented and the Camel's neck was thrust within the tent.

He stood, moving his head from side to side uneasily, and presently said: "It is awkward standing thus. It would take but a little more room if I were to place my forelegs inside the tent."

"You may place your forelegs within the tent," said the Arab. And now he had to move a little to make room, for the tent was small.

The Camel spoke again: "I keep the tent open by standing thus, and make it cold for us both. May I not stand wholly within?"

"Yes," said the Arab, whose compassion included his beast as well as himself, "come in wholly if you wish." But now the tent proved to be too small to hold both.

"I think, after all," said the Camel, as he crowded himself in, "that there will not be room here for us both. You are the smaller; it will be best for you to stand outside. There will be room then for me." So he pushed a little, and the Arab with all haste went outside the tent.

The Spider and the Fly
by Mary Howitt

"Will you walk into my parlour?" said the Spider to the Fly,
"'Tis the prettiest little parlour that ever you did spy;
The way into my parlour is up a winding stair,
And I've a many curious things to shew when you are there."
"Oh no, no," said the little Fly, "to ask me is in vain,
For who goes up your winding stair can ne'er come down again."

"I'm sure you must be weary, dear, with soaring up so high;
Will you rest upon my little bed?" said the Spider to the Fly.
"There are pretty curtains drawn around; the sheets are fine and thin,
And if you like to rest awhile, I'll snugly tuck you in!"
"Oh no, no," said the little Fly, "for I've often heard it said,
They never, never wake again, who sleep upon your bed!"

Said the cunning Spider to the Fly, "Dear friend what can I do,
To prove the warm affection I've always felt for you?
I have within my pantry, good store of all that's nice;
I'm sure you're very welcome—will you please to take a slice?"
"Oh no, no," said the little Fly, "kind Sir, that cannot be,
I've heard what's in your pantry, and I do not wish to see!"

"Sweet creature!" said the Spider, "you're witty and you're wise,
How handsome are your gauzy wings, how brilliant are your eyes!
I've a little looking-glass upon my parlour shelf,
If you'll step in one moment, dear, you shall behold yourself."
"I thank you, gentle sir," she said, "for what you're pleased to say,
And bidding you good morning now, I'll call another day."

The Spider turned him round about, and went into his den,
For well he knew the silly Fly would soon come back again:
So he wove a subtle web, in a little corner sly,
And set his table ready, to dine upon the Fly.
Then he came out to his door again, and merrily did sing,
"Come hither, hither, pretty Fly, with the pearl and silver wing;
Your robes are green and purple—there's a crest upon your head;
Your eyes are like the diamond bright, but mine are dull as lead!"

Alas, alas! how very soon this silly little Fly,
Hearing his wily, flattering words, came slowly flitting by;
With buzzing wings she hung aloft, then near and nearer drew,
Thinking only of her brilliant eyes, and green and purple hue—
Thinking only of her crested head—poor foolish thing! At last,
Up jumped the cunning Spider, and fiercely held her fast.
He dragged her up his winding stair, into his dismal den,
Within his little parlour—but she ne'er came out again!

And now dear little children, who may this story read,
To idle, silly flattering words, I pray you ne'er give heed:
Unto an evil counsellor, close heart and ear and eye,
And take a lesson from this tale, of the Spider and the Fly.

Copywork

Narration

Instructor: Write or print part of today's narration to use as copywork.

103. Nouns and Pronouns as Adjectives

- This Week: A Wonder-Book for Girls and Boys: The Miraculous Pitcher

Did you know that sometimes, nouns and pronouns can act as adjectives? You've already learned about one example of this: possessive nouns and pronouns! Remember that when we want to show possession with a noun, we add an **apostrophe s** (**'s**) to the noun. When we want to show possession with a pronoun, we just use the possessive pronouns: (first person) my, mine, our, ours, (second person) your, yours, (third person) his, her, hers, its, their, theirs.

Old Philemon and his old wife Baucis sat at their cottage-door.

"I do wish our neighbors felt a little more kindness for their fellow-creatures."

But, in my private opinion, old Philemon's eyesight had been playing him tricks again.

In the sentences from The Miraculous Pitcher above, the underlined words are acting as adjectives because they modify nouns.

There are many other times when we use nouns as adjectives to modify another noun. The word **soccer** is a noun because it is the name of a thing—a game. When I say **soccer ball**, I'm no longer speaking of the game, I'm speaking of the ball. If I just said **ball**, you wouldn't know what kind of ball I meant. But when I modify **ball** with **soccer**, you know exactly what kind of ball! Look at the sentences below. Which nouns are acting as adjectives?

The boy bought potato chips.

She used a paper towel to clean the mess.

The baby played with a toy dinosaur.

There Was a Cherry-Tree
by James Whitcomb Riley

There was a cherry-tree. Its bloomy snows
Cool even now the fevered sight that knows
No more its airy visions of pure joy —
As when you were a boy.

There was a cherry-tree. The Bluejay sat
His blue against its white — O blue as jet
He seemed there then!— But now — Whoever knew
He was so pale a blue!

There was a cherry-tree — our child-eyes saw
The miracle:— Its pure white snows did thaw
Into a crimson fruitage, far too sweet
But for a boy to eat.

There was a cherry-tree, give thanks and joy!—
There was a bloom of snow — There was a boy —
There was a bluejay of the realest blue —
And fruit for both of you.

The Hen and the Swallow
An Aesop's Fable retold by J. H. Stickney

A Hen who had no nest of her own found some eggs, and, in the kindness of her heart, thought she would take care of them, and keep them warm.

But they were the eggs of a viper; and by and by the little snakes began to come out of the shell.

A Swallow, who was passing, stopped to look at them.

"What a foolish creature you were, to hatch those eggs!" said the Swallow. "Don't you know that as soon as the little snakes grow big enough, they will bite some one— probably you first of all?"

"Then," said the Hen, as she stood on one leg and looked at the ugly little snakes, first with one eye and then with the other, "you think I have done more harm then good?"

"I certainly do," said the Swallow, as she flew away. "Good judgment is better than thoughtless kindness."

Exercise

In your workbook, underline the noun and the pronoun acting as adjectives from this passage:

> Their food was seldom anything but bread, milk, and vegetables, and now and then a bunch of grapes that had ripened against the cottage wall.

Label them as adjectives ADJ because that's what they are in these sentences!

Copywork

Literature

Their food was seldom anything but bread, milk, and vegetables, and now and then a bunch of grapes that had ripened against the cottage wall.

Poetry—Maker of Heaven and Earth

The tall trees in the greenwood,
The meadows where we play,
The rushes by the water,
We gather every day.

104. Nouns and Pronouns as Adjectives

- This Week: A Wonder-Book for Girls and Boys: The Miraculous Pitcher

In each of the following sentences from "The Miraculous Pitcher," there is a noun acting as an adjective. Which noun is acting as an adjective in each sentence? Which noun is being modified?

There, fishes had glided to and fro in the depths, and water-weeds had grown along the margin.

They would only have laughed, had anybody told them that human beings owe a debt of love to one another.

"Those children (the little rascals!) have bespattered us finely with their mud-balls."

But, undoubtedly, here was the grandest figure that ever sat so humbly beside a cottage door.

In the first sentence, **water** modifies **weeds**. In the second sentence, **human** modifies **beings**. In the third sentence, **mud** modifies **balls**. And in the fourth sentence, **cottage** modifies **door**.

Wynken, Blynken, and Nod
by Eugene Field

Wynken, Blynken, and Nod one night
Sailed off in a wooden shoe—
Sailed on a river of crystal light,
Into a sea of dew.
"Where are you going, and what do you wish?"
The old moon asked the three.
"We have come to fish for the herring fish
That live in this beautiful sea;
Nets of silver and gold have we!"
Said Wynken,
Blynken,
And Nod.

The old moon laughed and sang a song,
As they rocked in the wooden shoe,
And the wind that sped them all night long
Ruffled the waves of dew.
The little stars were the herring fish
That lived in that beautiful sea—
"Now cast your nets wherever you wish—
Never afeard are we";
So cried the stars to the fishermen three:
Wynken,
Blynken,
And Nod.

All night long their nets they threw
To the stars in the twinkling foam—
Then down from the skies came the wooden shoe,
Bringing the fishermen home;
'Twas all so pretty a sail it seemed
As if it could not be,
And some folks thought 'twas a dream they'd dreamed
Of sailing that beautiful sea—
But I shall name you the fishermen three:
Wynken,
Blynken,
And Nod.

Wynken and Blynken are two little eyes,
And Nod is a little head,
And the wooden shoe that sailed the skies
Is a wee one's trundle-bed.
So shut your eyes while mother sings
Of wonderful sights that be,
And you shall see the beautiful things
As you rock in the misty sea,
Where the old shoe rocked the fishermen three:
Wynken,
Blynken,
And Nod.

A Fox and a Crab
An Aesop's Fable retold by J. H. Stickney

A hungry Fox surprised a Crab, who had left the sea and was lying upon the beach.

"What good luck, to find a breakfast so easily," said the Fox, as he pounced upon him.

"Well," said the Crab, when he found that he was to be eaten, "this comes of going where I have no business; I should have stayed in the water, where I belonged."

Exercise

In your workbook, underline the noun and the pronoun acting as adjectives from this passage:

> The milk pitcher, I must not forget to say, retained its marvelous quality of being never empty when it was desirable to have it full.

Label them as adjectives ADJ because that's what they are in these sentences!

Copywork

Literature

> The milk pitcher, I must not forget to say, retained its marvelous quality of being never empty when it was desirable to have it full.

Bible—Galatians 5:22-23

> But the fruit of the Spirit is love, joy, peace, patience, kindness, goodness, faithfulness, gentleness, self-control; against such things there is no law.

Village Street and Stairs with Figures by Vincent Van Gogh

Picture Study

1. Read the title and the name of the artist. Study the picture for several minutes, then put the picture away.

2. Describe the picture.

3. Look at the picture again. Do you notice any details that you missed before? What do you like or dislike about this painting? Does it remind you of anything?

105. Review: Synonyms; Picture Study: Village Street and Stairs

- This Week: A Wonder-Book for Girls and Boys: The Miraculous Pitcher

Synonyms are words that have the same meaning.

Remember that synonyms are words that have the same meaning, like large and huge, or thin and skinny.

Read "My Shadow" by Robert Louis Stevenson. Can you think of a synonym for each of the underlined words in the first stanza?

My Shadow
by Robert Louis Stevenson

I have a <u>little</u> shadow that goes <u>in</u> and <u>out</u> with me,
And what can be the use of him is more than I can see.
He is very, very <u>like</u> me from the heels up to the <u>head</u>;
And I see him <u>jump</u> before me, when I jump into my bed.

The funniest thing about him is the way he likes to grow—
Not at all like proper children, which is always very slow;
For he sometimes shoots up taller like an india-rubber ball,
And he sometimes goes so little that there's none of him at all.

He hasn't got a notion of how children ought to play,
And can only make a fool of me in every sort of way.
He stays so close behind me, he's a coward you can see;
I'd think shame to stick to nursie as that shadow sticks to me!

One morning, very early, before the sun was up,
I rose and found the shining dew on every buttercup;
But my lazy little shadow, like an arrant sleepy-head,
Had stayed at home behind me and was fast asleep in bed.

Exercise

In your workbook, label the nouns N and the adjectives ADJ from this passage:

> "My good wife Baucis has gone to see what you can have for supper. We are poor folks; but you shall be welcome to whatever we have in the cupboard."

Remember that articles are adjectives, so label them adj.

Copywork

Literature

> "My good wife Baucis has gone to see what you can have for supper. We are poor folks; but you shall be welcome to whatever we have in the cupboard."

106. Review: Commas in a Series

- This Week: A Wonder-Book for Girls and Boys: The Chimæra

Conjunctions are words that join words or groups of words together. Remember that sometimes, we might have a long list of words to join together. Instead of using the conjunction **and** so many times, we can use commas.

>On our farm, we have chickens <u>and</u> ducks <u>and</u> goats <u>and</u> a cow.
>On our farm, we have chickens, ducks, goats, and a cow.

In the following sentence from "The Chimæra," there are two separate lists joined by commas.

>It had a tail like a boa-constrictor, its body was like I do not care what, and it had three separate heads, one of which was a lion's, the second a goat's, and the third an abominably great snake's.

Can you identify the groups of words joined together by commas in the sentence above?

Note that each word or group of words in our list except for the last one is followed by a comma instead of the conjunction **and**. We only use the conjunction **and** before the last word or group of words in our list.

Make a sentence that has a list of more than two items. You might want to choose to list your favorite things, things you like to do, or your favorite books. Ask your instructor to write your sentence in your workbook, and tell your instructor where to place the commas!

Certainty
by Emily Dickinson

I never saw a moor,
I never saw the sea;
Yet know I how the heather looks,
And what a wave must be.

I never spoke with God,
Nor visited in heaven;
Yet certain am I of the spot
As if the chart were given.

The Fox and the Goat
An Aesop's Fable retold by J. H. Stickney

A Fox once happened to fall into a deep well. He tried in every way to get out, but at last began to think that it was impossible, and that he must die there, a prisoner. While he was thinking how sad that would be, a thirsty Goat came and looked down into the well, wishing that he could get some water. He soon saw the Fox.

"Halloo," said the Goat, "what are you doing down there? Is the water good?"

"The best I ever tasted," answered the Fox. "It is cool, and clear, and delicious. Come down and try it yourself."

"I will," said the Goat, "for I am nearly dead with thirst."

So he jumped down, and drank as much water as he wanted.

"Oh, how refreshing!" cried he.

"Yes," said the Fox. "And now, if you have finished drinking, let me ask how you expect to get out of this well again."

"Oh, I don't know," replied the Goat. "How do you expect to get out?"

"That is what I have been wondering about for the last hour," said the Fox, "and have just now thought of a good plan. If you will put your forefeet high up on the wall, I will climb up your back, and so get out, and then, of course, I can help you out."

"Very well," said the Goat, who was a simple creature, "that is a good plan. How I wish I had your brains!" He put his forefeet on the wall, and the Fox easily climbed out and started to go on his way.

"Wait a moment," called the Goat. "You forgot to help me out."

"You foolish fellow!" said the Fox, with a mocking laugh. "You ought to have thought how you would get out before you jumped down. I fell in, but you went down of your own accord. Look before you leap next time." And off he ran.

Exercise

In your workbook, label the verbs V, linking verbs LV, and adverbs ADV from this passage:

He was as wild, as swift, and as buoyant in his flight through the air as any eagle that ever soared into the clouds.

Copywork

Literature

He was as wild, as swift, and as buoyant in his flight through the air as any eagle that ever soared into the clouds.

Poetry—Maker of Heaven and Earth

He gave us eyes to see them,
And lips that we might tell
How great is God Almighty,
Who has made all things well.

107. The Eight Parts of Speech

- This Week: A Wonder-Book for Girls and Boys: The Chimæra

The parts of speech are the eight different types of words that we use to communicate. Today, you're going to learn the definitions of all eight parts of speech!

Are you ready? The eight parts of speech are nouns, pronouns, verbs, adjectives, adverbs, prepositions, conjunctions, and interjections. Now for the definitions...

What? Are you saying you already know the definitions for the eight parts of speech? Then I guess I don't have to teach them to you today! Instead, you can just recite each definition.

The Window
by Walter de la Mare

Behind the blinds I sit and watch
The people passing—passing by;
And not a single one can see
   My tiny watching eye.

They cannot see my little room,
All yellowed with the shaded sun;
They do not even know I'm here;
   Nor'll guess when I am gone.

The Ant and the Dove
An Aesop's Fable retold by J. H. Stickney

An Ant, walking by the river one day, said to himself, "How nice and cool this water looks! I must drink some of it." But as he began to drink, his foot slipped, and he fell in.
"Oh, somebody please help me, or I shall drown!" cried he.
A dove, sitting in a tree that overhung the river, heard him, and threw him a leaf. "Climb up on that leaf," said she, "and you will float ashore."

The Ant climbed up onto the leaf, which the wind blew to the shore, and he stepped upon dry land again.

"Good-by, kind Dove," said he, as he ran home. "You have saved my life, and I wish I could do something for you."

"Good-by," said the Dove. "Be careful not to fall in again."

A few days after this, when the Dove was busy building her nest, the Ant saw a man just raising his gun to shoot her.

He ran quickly, and bit the man's leg so hard that he cried, "Oh! Oh!" and dropped his gun.

This startled the Dove and she flew away. The man picked up his gun, and walked away.

When he was gone, the Dove came back to her nest.

"Thank you, my little friend," she said. "You have saved my life."

And the little Ant was overjoyed to think he had been able to do for the Dove what the Dove had so lately done for him.

Exercise

In your workbook, see how many of the words you can label with the correct part of speech from this passage:

> "And one other time, as I was coming to the fountain with my pitcher, I heard a neigh."

The sentence doesn't have all the parts of speech. How many parts of speech does it have?

Noun N, verb V, linking verb LV, pronoun PRO, adjective ADJ, adverb ADV, preposition PREP, conjunction CJ, interjection INJ.

Copywork

Literature

> "And one other time, as I was coming to the fountain with my pitcher, I heard a neigh."

Maxim

> Early to bed, early to rise,
> Makes a man healthy, wealthy, and wise.

108. Narration: The Town Mouse and the Country Mouse

- **This Week: A Wonder-Book for Girls and Boys: The Chimæra**

It's time for a narration. Your instructor will read this fable to you, and you will tell the story back to her while she writes it down for you. Then your instructor will write part of it for you to use as copywork.

The Town Mouse and the Country Mouse
An Aesop's Fable

A Town Mouse once visited a relative who lived in the country. For lunch the Country Mouse served wheat stalks, roots, and acorns, with a dash of cold water for drink. The Town Mouse ate very sparingly, nibbling a little of this and a little of that, and by her manner making it very plain that she ate the simple food only to be polite.

After the meal the friends had a long talk, or rather the Town Mouse talked about her life in the city while the Country Mouse listened. They then went to bed in a cozy nest in the hedgerow and slept in quiet and comfort until morning. In her sleep the Country Mouse dreamed she was a Town Mouse with all the luxuries and delights of city life that her friend had described for her. So the next day when the Town Mouse asked the Country Mouse to go home with her to the city, she gladly said yes.

When they reached the mansion in which the Town Mouse lived, they found on the table in the dining room the leavings of a very fine banquet. There were sweetmeats and jellies, pastries, delicious cheeses, indeed, the most tempting foods that a Mouse can imagine. But just as the Country Mouse was about to nibble a dainty bit of pastry, she heard a Cat mew loudly and scratch at the door. In great fear the Mice scurried to a hiding place, where they lay quite still for a long time, hardly daring to breathe. When at last they ventured back to the feast, the door opened suddenly and in came the servants to clear the table, followed by the House Dog.

The Country Mouse stopped in the Town Mouse's den only long enough to pick up her carpet bag and umbrella.

"You may have luxuries and dainties that I have not," she said as she hurried away, "but I prefer my plain food and simple life in the country with the peace and security that go with it."

Poverty with security is better than plenty in the midst of fear and uncertainty.

The City Mouse Lives in a House
by Christina Rossetti

The city mouse lives in a house;-
The garden mouse lives in a bower,
He's friendly with the frogs and toads,
And sees the pretty plants in flower.

The city mouse eats bread and cheese;-
The garden mouse eats what he can;
We will not grudge him seeds and stalks,
Poor little timid furry man.

Copywork

Narration

Instructor: Write or print part of today's narration to use as copywork.

The Man in the Moon
by James Whitcomb Riley

Said the Raggedy Man, on a hot afternoon:
    "My!
        Sakes!
            What a lot o' mistakes
Some little folks makes on The Man in the Moon!
But people that's b'en to see him like me,
And calls on him frequent and intimutly,
Might drop a few facts that would interest you
    Clean!
        Through!-
            If you wanted 'em to-
Some actual facts that might interest you!

"O The Man in the Moon has a crick in his back;
    Whee!
        Whimm!
            Aint you sorry for him?
And a mole on his nose that is purple and black;
And his eyes are so weak that they water and run
If he dares to dream even he looks at the sun-
So he jes' dreams of stars, as the doctors advise-
    My!
        Eyes!
            But isn't he wise-
To jes' dream of stars, as the doctors advise?

"And the Man in the Moon has a boil on his ear-
    Whee!
        Whing!
            What a singular thing!
I know! but these facts are authentic, my dear-
There's a boil on his ear; and a corn on his chin-
He calls it a dimple-but dimples stick in
Yet it might be a dimple turned over, you know!
    Whang!
        Ho!
            Why, certainly so!-
It might be a dimple turned over, you know!

"And The Man in the Moon has a rheumatic knee-
    Gee!
        Whizz!
            What a pity that is!
And his toes have worked round where his heels ought to be-
So whenever he wants to go North he goes South,
And comes back with porridge-crumbs all round his mouth,
And he brushes them off with a Japanese fan,
    Whing!
        Whann!
            What a marvelous man!
What a very remarkably marvelous man!

And the Man in the Moon, "sighed The Raggedy Man,
    "Gits!
        So!
            Sullonesome, you know-
Up there by hisse'f sence creation began!-
That when I call on him and then come away,
He grabs me and holds me and begs me to stay-
Till-Well! if it wasn't fer Jimmy-cum-jim,
    Dadd!
        Limb!
            I'd go pardners with him-
Jes' jump my job here and be pardners with him!"

Appendix A: Memory Work

A noun is the name of a person, place, thing, or idea.

The months of the year are January, February, March, April, May, June, July, August, September, October, November, and December.

A verb is a word that shows action or state of being.

A pronoun is a word used in the place of a noun.

    The first person pronouns are: I, me, my, mine, we, us, our, ours.

    The second person pronouns are: you, your, yours.

    The third person pronouns are: he, him, his, she, her, hers, it, its, they, them, their, theirs.

An antecedent is the noun that a pronoun replaces.

Homophones are words that have the same pronunciation but different meanings.

The four seasons are winter, spring, summer, and fall.

Home Address

Phone Number

The state of being verbs are: am, are, is, was, were, be, being, been.

The linking verbs are: am, are, is, was, were, be, being, been, become, seem.

The helping verbs are:
am, are, is,	was, were,	be, being, been,
do, does, did,	have, has, had,	may, might, must,
can, could,	shall, should,	will, would

The days of the week are Sunday, Monday, Tuesday, Wednesday, Thursday, Friday, and Saturday.

A conjunction is a word that joins words or groups of words together.

A sentence is a group of words that expresses a complete thought.

The Four Types of Sentences:

    A declarative sentence makes a statement. It ends with a period.

    An interrogative sentence asks a question. It ends with a question mark.

    An exclamatory sentence shows sudden or strong feeling. It ends with an exclamation mark.

    An imperative sentence gives a command or makes a request. It ends with a period.

An adjective is a word that modifies a noun or a pronoun.

A preposition is a word that shows the relationship between a noun or a pronoun and another word in the sentence.

Some of the most common prepositions are:
> aboard, about, above, across, after, against, along, among, around, at,
> before, behind, below, beneath, beside, between, beyond, by,
> down, during, except, for, from, in, inside, into, like, near, of, off,
> on, onto, outside, over, past, round, since, through, throughout, till, to, toward,
> under, underneath, until, up, upon, with, within, without.

(Please see Appendix B: Memorizing Prepositions, Pros and Cons.)

An interjection is a word or group of words that shows sudden or strong feeling.

An adverb is a word that modifies a verb, an adjective, or another adverb.

Antonyms are words that have opposite meanings.

The articles are a, an, the. Articles are adjectives.

Synonyms are words that have the same meaning.

Appendix B: Memorizing Prepositions, Pros and Cons

The main argument for memorizing a list of the most common prepositions is that it will make them easy for children to spot in sentences.

That also happens to be the main argument against memorizing a list. The problem is that many of the most common prepositions can also function as other parts of speech. By memorizing a list, we are stating, "These are prepositions." Then, a child sees **up** acting as an adverb. My question is: What effect will the learned list have then? Will the child ignore other instruction and focus on the list? Or will he think it through and remember that the words on the list aren't **only** prepositions.

Some would argue that most children will not have any problems with this. That leads to a second question: What about all of the other prepositions? Most lists of prepositions only include the most common ones, about 50-60. There are almost 100 one-word prepositions. There are another 50 or so prepositions that have two or more words. In order to spot these, the children have to understand what prepositions are, and if they understand that, they don't need the list. That leads to question number three, one for which I have no answer: Will the list help or hinder children when they encounter new prepositions?

All of this leads to the fourth question: What good will it do? Understanding prepositions is enough. When I wrote the first Language Lessons book for my second son, I believed that it was best for children to memorize the list, but we never actually did it. My oldest son also never memorized the list. And yet, they've both been able to find them in sentences. They both diagram prepositions without having to flip through a mental list first. So can I. So can many people.

In the end, enough people have children memorize prepositions for me to assume that it does no harm. But experience, ours and that of others, says that it's also not necessary. Because the lists memorized are usually incomplete, and because so many common prepositions also function frequently as other parts of speech, we choose not to memorize. However, a list of common prepositions is included for those who feel differently.

Made in the USA
Lexington, KY
19 April 2017